SPECTATOR IN
HELL

A British soldier's story
of imprisonment in Auschwitz

COLIN RUSHTON

summersdale

SPECTATOR IN HELL

First published by Pharoah Press in 1998
Second edition published in 2001 by Summersdale Publishers Ltd,
reprinted 2005

This edition published in 2007 by Summersdale Publishers Ltd

Summersdale Publishers Ltd
46 West Street
Chichester
West Sussex
PO19 1RP
UK

www.summersdale.com

Printed and bound Great Britain

ISBN: 1-84024-614-6
ISBN 13: 978-1-84024-614-8

ACKNOWLEDGEMENTS

With thanks to the Wiener Library for supplying photographs 1 and 2 and to the National Archives and Records Administration for photograph 5 (reference number 208-YE-193).

Thanks are due to Duncan Little, a journalist and researcher, for the many hours spent searching the National Archives for vital supporting facts to ratify Arthur Dodd's story.

Thank you to The National Archives for allowing us reference to their records for verification purposes, the more than one hundred miles of shelving holding no less than nine million documents.

Although every effort has been made to trace the present copyright holders, we apologise in advance for any unintentional omission or neglect and will be pleased to insert appropriate acknowledgement to companies or individuals in any subsequent edition of this publication.

Other books by the same author:

Beyond the Gates of Hell
Spirit of the Trenches

CONTENTS

PROLOGUE

The train ground to a halt and the sliding doors of the carriage crashed open. The two dozen men inside raised their hands to the sun and in turn jumped down from the train. They were met by a chorus of commands from the handful of Wehrmacht guards awaiting their arrival.

'Bewegen sie! Bewegen! Schnell!'

Falling into some semblance of a formation, the men slowly grew accustomed to the bright daylight after several hours in the dark and took in the scene before them. Their eyes were met by a vision of rural tranquillity. To the right, fields of yellow clay rolled into the distance and to the left was a romantic little copse, a perfect retreat for a courting couple.

There were no factories in sight and no building work was in evidence. From where they stood there was no sign of any industry taking place at all. They had crossed the German border the night before and guessed they were probably now in Poland. Discussing their new location quietly among themselves, the consensus of opinion was that they were destined for farmwork. As prison camp work went, this was good news; they would have plenty of fresh air and there should at least be an abundance of fresh fruit and vegetables to eat.

SPECTATOR IN HELL

Looking down the length of the train, Arthur noticed hundreds of bundles a yard or so from the track. There were trousers, shirts, skirts and shoes, some clearly belonging to young children. Only mildly curious, he thought little of it; he was far too relieved that his worst fears regarding their destination had not been realised.

A short march brought them to a camp and if Arthur felt any apprehension as he entered the gates, it soon disappeared. Inside the perimeter fence were ten wooden huts. The POWs were ushered into the nearest and they were pleasantly surprised by how dry and clean it was. Further investigation revealed central heating pipes running the length of the hut, hot and cold running water at each basin and solid bunk-beds, upon which were clean and adequate mattresses.

For the next two weeks the men settled themselves into what they hoped would be their accommodation for the rest of the war and, in the spring of 1943, it was anybody's guess how long that would be.

A week later, Arthur woke slowly to the noise of guards stomping through the hut's central corridor, banging rifle-butts on doors. Over the past few days the number of British prisoners in the camp had swollen from two dozen to nearer two hundred, but they had been required to do little or no work and had been reasonably well-fed.

The guards were smiling and enjoying themselves, but there was no friendship in it. There was something sinister happening and they were about to find out what it was.

'Der Feiertag endig! Arbeiten sie jetzt!'

Those who had more than a smattering of the language were asked what was being said and Arthur learned that they were being sent to work. Knowing this moment would come sooner or later, the men shrugged and made their way out to the parade area.

Once gathered into formation, they were marched out of the camp and along a dusty road running through a forest. Arthur, with his mates, was up at the front. On route they came across a group of prisoners working to one side of the road. They were Ukrainian women digging ditches under the watchful eye of several armed guards carrying coiled whips. The fear and tension in the women's eyes was tangible. Prior to their arrival the men had been at Farasabrina in Italy and Arthur had drawn the lowest card and missed out on what turned out to be a fairly straightforward escape bid. He wondered now how much he would regret that.

A few minutes later they came to a factory. To the side of the road was a young girl of about fifteen being severely and brutally flogged with a riding crop by an officer of the SS. Kneeling helplessly in front of him, the young girl was facing the oncoming POWs and presented to them a figure of terror. Her hair had been carelessly shaven and her scalp was cut. Fresh wounds inflicted by the German officer were bleeding and small red rivers ran from her forehead to her chin.

She was naked above the waist and Arthur could see from her ribs and drawn cheeks that she had not been properly fed for some time. The officer momentarily stopped for breath and the young girl looked up. Her eyes were saucepan-wide as she pleaded to the sadistic monster before her to relent. He laughed out loud and shouted across to two of the guards standing by. Then he carried on mercilessly whipping her across the head and shoulders.

For some of the Tommies watching it was too much. One of the lads tapped Arthur on the shoulder and stepped forward.

'Come on, lads,' he said, 'I've had enough of this little bastard!'

Arthur and three others followed him, walking purposefully towards the SS officer. Arthur shouted for him to leave the girl alone. Unused to such a challenge to his authority, the officer was momentarily taken aback, but as they closed in he took the whip into his left hand and reached for his pistol. At the same time, a soldier of the Wehrmacht raised his rifle and aimed it at the men. The soldier's call stopped them in their tracks.

'Anhalten sie! Er werde getut!'

Translation was hardly necessary; if they took another step, the officer would shoot them dead. There was no camaraderie between the two Germans. What the soldier was telling them was for their own good.

'Zuruchgehen sie!'

The men stopped and the officer smiled across to the rifle-bearing soldier. Still holding his pistol, he walked towards the Tommies.

As it was Arthur who had shouted out, he stood in front of him and stared coldly into his eyes. The officer was the prototype of Hitler's Aryan Adonis: tall, handsome, blond and steely-blue eyed. Arthur dared to stare him out, his own revulsion of the man overcoming the fear he felt. Without dropping his cynical smile, the officer nodded and backed away.

'*Ein anderer Zeit,*' he whispered to Arthur with menace; 'Another time.'

Arthur was in no doubt that they would meet again before very long. Orders were barked and the men were ordered back into the column. Marching again, they looked behind them and saw their intervention had done the girl no favours. The officer beat her now with a greater ferocity than ever. Arthur clenched his fists and grimaced. He knew that her only crime was to be Jewish. She would not live much longer.

Arthur woke with a start, his body trembling and sweating. The nightmare was frightening and familiar. It was one of a number he had endured for nigh-on forty years. His wife, Olwen, had long ago become used to his sudden screams in the night. She got up without comment and made her way downstairs to the kitchen. A few minutes later, she came back with a cup of tea and a couple of aspirins as she always did. She held a vinegar-soaked flannel to his forehead and murmured her usual words of comfort.

'Same old nightmare again, love?'

Arthur nodded, but this was much more than a nightmare. He was reliving an incident from which he had never mentally recovered. In 1943, Arthur had been captured and sent to a succession of prisoner of war camps before being interned just outside a small Polish town for nearly two years. When the war was over, he had tried to talk about his experiences, but found it very difficult to describe what he had seen. In any case, he knew that few people would believe him; there were no Tommies there, only Jews.

But Arthur had been there. The camp was near a beautiful village in Upper Silesia known to the local Poles as Oswiecim. The Germans gave it another name, now synonymous with mankind's most perverse and darkest hours.

They called it Auschwitz.

PART ONE: ARTHUR'S STORY

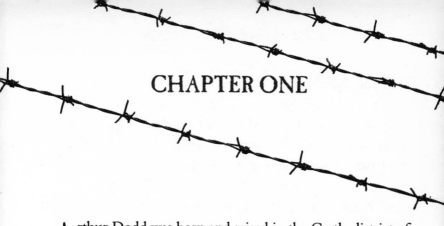

CHAPTER ONE

Arthur Dodd was born and raised in the Castle district of Northwich, a small Cheshire town on the River Weaver. His mother's first husband had been killed in the trenches of France during World War One and she had married his father, a regular soldier in the Cheshire Regiment, just after Armistice Day. Arthur himself arrived on 7 December 1919.

His father was an austere, distant man. He had served in the Boer War at the turn of the century and as a sergeant had been captured during the Great War. As a parent, he was distinctly military and Victorian in his attitude and had little time for Arthur and his younger sister.

At fifteen, Arthur left school and was taken on as an apprentice mechanic at Northwich Transport Company. There he learned to drive and began to understand the mechanics of the internal combustion engine under the watchful, friendly eye of his boss, Harold Isherwood. For his labours he was paid all of ten shillings (fifty pence) a week.

The company owned a Ford People's Popular saloon car, which was used to transport mechanics to broken-down lorries. Arthur fell in love with it the first time he saw it. It was in this car he was taught to drive and, having added a year to his age when completing the driving licence application form, he passed his test in the early part of 1935. A year later, he repeated the lie and passed his HGV test.

Those early working days were fun for Arthur. Harold took to the young man and they would often go fishing together in one of the many meres in the Cheshire countryside. Arthur had to serve under the Articles of Apprenticeship for seven years, but when Harold opened his own transport company in 1937, he invited Arthur to finish his time with him.

Tempted though he was, ten shillings a week was hardly conducive to living away from home and Arthur had to decline. Also, his mother was against it, as she was the transport business in general. In those days a driver had to find his own consignments and could be away from home for as long as three weeks at a time.

In Harold's absence, Arthur quickly became bored and began looking for another company to take him on. When he was eighteen he entered the world of scrap, being employed as a driver by Jimmy Caffrey, a well-respected local entrepreneur. Caffrey only had one vehicle and most of the work was sub-contracted from the Middlewich Borough Council. Consequently, Arthur was home every night by tea-time and was paid the quite princely sum of five pounds a week.

Caffrey was a decent man and would often make his lorry available to transport local people to Clatterbridge Hospital on the Wirral. For this extra work, he paid Arthur five shillings, half of what he earned at the Northwich Transport Company for a full week. For many, Caffrey's lorry was the only way they could get to the hospital to visit sick relatives, but he never objected to those who jumped aboard for the day out.

'Take your mum along,' he used to say to Arthur. 'The run will do her good.'

Despite Caffrey's generosity and kindness, Mrs Dodd was still unhappy about the driving her son had to do and finally persuaded him to join the Weaver Navigation Company. His grandfather had sailed on the Salt Union boats and his Uncle Jack was a foreman there. To please his mother, Arthur had to give up his beloved driving and also take a serious cut in wages. At the WNC he started on just one guinea (one pound, five pence) a week, rising to thirty-eight shillings (one pound, ninety pence) when he was twenty-one.

He gave most of his wages to his mother, as he had done when he worked for Caffrey, so in fact it was she who suffered as much as anyone with his loss of income. She was, though, more concerned with his long term prospects and saw security and advancement in his new position.

For three months, he was employed over at Weston Point, Runcorn, where the building of a number of clay sheds was being completed. He had to ride the 13 miles to work each day on an old 'sit up and beg' lady's bicycle and when the wind was against him the journey could take as long as an hour and a half. Adults were allowed nine pence a day for travel expenses, but Arthur, under twenty-one, received only sixpence. As the return bus fare was nine pence, the road between Runcorn and Northwich was always busy with young lads pedalling their way to work and back.

In 1938, developments in Germany began to look ominous and talk of another war was in the air. Hitler had been in power for five years and in March Germany had annexed

Austria. Ned Bebbington, a good mate of Arthur's at the WNC, had decided to join the Territorial Army. Arthur was encouraged to do the same, but his mother's response was an emphatic 'No'. Frightened by the ever-increasing probability of war, she knew the Territorials would be the first to be called up and wanted her one and only precious son at home for as long as possible. (As it happened, Ned became a sergeant with the Cheshires and spent the entire war as an officers' mess manager in Northern Ireland!)

Towards the end of the summer of 1938, Arthur was walking two girls along the riverbank near Hartford, in the company of his close friend, Alan Parks.

'I'm joining the Navy, Arthur,' Alan told him. 'Why don't you join up with me?'

Alan was caught up in the patriotic fervour sweeping the country, but Arthur, just short of his twentieth birthday, still needed his mother's permission and once again it was refused. The war was to be a sad time for the Parks family with both Alan and his brother, George, being killed. Alan lost his life aboard the HMS *Repulse* in Singapore, while George was shot down serving in the RAF.

In September of that same year, the governments of both France and Britain were seen by many to be weak in their stand against the growing demands and incursions of Nazi Germany. Hitler won a major concession when allowed to seize the Sudetenland, the Germanic quarter of Czechoslovakia, without resistance.

In the same month, it seemed that the possibility of Arthur taking an active part in any war that might break out had disappeared. He was helping to run a boat along its launch ramp when his left foot became trapped between the ramp and a turning wheel. It was some moments before the other members of the working party realised, by which time his foot was nearly severed; attached to his leg only by the sinews of his instep. His Achilles' tendon was severed and his heel severely crushed.

His foot was saved from amputation and stitched back together by a Dr Booth at the Northwich Infirmary, but he was bluntly told, as he endured a slow and painful recovery, that he would spend the rest of his life with a club foot. Each day he suffered a course of painful physiotherapy to stretch the Achilles' tendon and allow him to put his heel fully on the ground. At times the pain was unbearable, but in just six weeks he was fit enough to hobble back into work for light duties as a stocktaker in the company stores.

During the summer of 1939, and despite the efforts of government appeasers, Britain was dragged inextricably towards war. Finally, on 1 September, the German Army and the Luftwaffe invaded Poland in a ruthless and murderous blitzkrieg. There was no room left for negotiation. Hitler was ready for a European war and had thrown the gauntlet down. With nervous trepidation, Britain picked it up.

For Arthur, the first few months of war were a huge disappointment, but this was overtaken by grief in February 1940, when his mother died. She had contracted the influenza bug sweeping the country that winter and died of pleurisy. The linchpin of the family was gone, but she had departed this world happy in the knowledge that Arthur would take no active part in the war.

Throughout this time, with Dr Booth's assistance, Arthur's treatment continued. Arthur had never conceded that his injuries were permanent. The press was full of the country's urgent need for volunteers and Arthur broached the subject that he might try to join up. The doctor certainly knew that he had no chance of passing a full medical, but believed it was important that Arthur's mental attitude should remain positive.

'It might be a bit soon, Arthur, to be honest,' he told him, 'but why not go along and see? A country can ask no more of its young men than that they are willing.'

At the medical, he was examined by an orthopaedic specialist, a Dr Hay, who watched Arthur carefully as he stripped down to his underpants and walked nervously about the room. Dr Hay made his assessment and handed the report to the recruitment officer, a veteran of World War One who wore a scarlet sash across his chest and had a bushy, grey moustache. He looked over the results of Arthur's medical and slowly shook his head.

'I'm sorry, lad,' he said, 'but we can't take you. You've been assessed as a "B2" and I'm afraid that's not good enough.'

Seeing Arthur's obvious distress, he vainly tried to reassure him.

'Look, lad, this is not a permanent grade. Why don't you keep working at it and have another go in a year or two?'

Arthur looked at the floor and nodded in silence before turning away. He was about to pass through the exit door when the officer called after him.

'Hang on a minute, have you got a driving licence?'

He was obviously doing all he could to accommodate Arthur. Arthur replied that he had an HGV licence and the officer's face brightened.

'Well, lad, I don't know if we can give you a rifle, but you might come in handy as a driving instructor.'

He told him that the Army would be in touch soon. Arthur was lifted beyond words. At least he would be in uniform and doing his bit. He smiled to himself when he thought of his mother. He would be in the Army and back behind a steering wheel. She would have had a fit!

'Don't worry, Mum,' he said to himself, 'I'll be a long way from the fighting.'

CHAPTER TWO

The Army Drivers' Centre was located in Foundry Street in Whittington Moor, near Chesterfield and there were approximately 150 men billeted there. Corporal Saxby of the East Lancashire Regiment was in charge of the drill sessions, Colonel Cope was the technical advisor of mechanics and Sergeant Edwards was the weapons instructor. As driving instructors with Arthur were three retired London bus drivers, one of whom was called Sergeant Picket.

The vehicles used for instruction were three-ton Albion lorries with gate-change gears, but when the tuition started on the first morning, Arthur was instructed to line up with the other trainees. He was then crammed with half a dozen other men into one of the Albion cabs as each took it in turn to receive instruction. The session was fraught with danger. Most of the lads had never driven a motor car before, let alone a commercial transport vehicle. How nobody was killed was a mystery for which Arthur thanked the Lord at the end of the day.

When it was his turn, it was obvious that Arthur knew exactly what he was doing. Sergeant Picket gave him a long, hard look.

'What can you drive?' he asked him.

'Anything,' Arthur replied. 'I thought I was coming here to instruct, not be instructed!' The error was quickly rectified and later when Arthur was talking to Picket, the old man revealed that he had, in fact, been sent to the school to teach young officers to drive staff cars. For the purpose, the Army had provided an old Humber Snipe, but Picket told a startled Arthur that he had only ever been taught to drive a bus.

'You're pulling my leg!' Arthur laughed.

'I'm afraid not,' Picket answered, 'I was taught to drive on a London bus and I've never had the chance to drive anything else. I wouldn't know where to start.'

'Literally, I suppose,' joked Arthur. The thought of getting behind the wheel of a Snipe had always been pure fantasy for Arthur, so he was quick to seize the opportunity.

'Tell you what, why don't I teach you? If you can drive a bus, you'll pick up how to drive a car in no time. While you're getting the hang of it, I'll teach the officers to drive the Humber.'

The two became firm friends.

The men were drilled each day and although Arthur was excused physical training, he joined in whenever he could to maintain the programme of exercise recommended by Dr Booth before he left. The war and the idea of impending danger were never very far away from the thoughts of the trainees at the school and soon they would be taking their newly-acquired skills to the front lines around the world, supplying arms and carrying despatches. For Arthur, though, no such fears or excitement troubled him. His war, he thought, would be spent in the Peak District.

There were many laughs amid the tension endured by men about to go to war. On one occasion, a trainee driver by the name of Wilson sneezed on parade and blew his false teeth across the cinder-laden ground. Colonel Saxby had been in a foul mood all morning, but even he had to laugh.

'I know you are all impatient to get at the Germans,' he said, addressing the men generally, 'but it seems that Wilson here would like to get his teeth into them straight away!'

The company fell apart at Wilson's toothless grin as he chased after his dentures.

There were many different forms of entertainment at Whittington, not least of which were the regular visits of a blind man from the local British Legion club who was the local draughts champion. He took on, and beat, anybody who fancied their chances as long as they made a donation to the club's funds first.

After a month or so, Picket was rushed into hospital with severe stomach pains and within a few days had died of peritonitis. He had become a close friend in a short time and it hit Arthur hard. There were, though, dreadful things happening all over Europe and he had to put it behind him.

At the outbreak of the war, there was a national shortage of qualified drivers. Only six of the men sent to Whittington had ever driven before and fewer again had been at the wheel of a lorry. Consequently, Arthur's skill was much sought after. It was brought to his attention that the Army was asking for volunteer lorry drivers to go to France and help the British Expeditionary Force who were struggling to keep a foothold on the European mainland. The war was going badly and the Army was being pushed into the English Channel by the Wehrmacht's Panzer divisions.

Germany had seized both Norway and Denmark in April 1940 and a month later the British Prime Minister, Neville Chamberlain, resigned. For some time, Chamberlain had committed his government to a policy of averting war and, having failed so completely, was left with little choice but to stand down. A coalition government was formed and Winston Churchill became Prime Minister, but the situation in France did not improve. Belgium was invaded and by the end of May many believed that an invasion of the south coast of England was both inevitable and imminent. They were dark days.

The absolute priority at that time for the War Office was to rescue as much of the BEF as was humanly possible. A huge flotilla of small seafaring craft bobbed across the channel in a seemingly endless roll, bringing back as many men as they could carry. On the French coast, the situation was desperate. In order to assist an orderly retreat, the Army needed drivers and Arthur volunteered to go. In such a time of crisis, his incapacity was almost irrelevant.

Late one evening, he was taken south and lodged in a large textile warehouse where he stayed for two nights. He did not have the remotest idea where he was. He was joined there by others from various units stationed around the country and the surface calm belied the nervous apprehension in everyone's heart. There was little or no news coming back from the continent and they were almost totally dependent on rumour and hearsay. Such was the tension on the second night that one man lost his nerve completely and began to discharge his rifle. Three men were shot, one of whom died. The broken man was finally overcome and led away, but the incident did nothing to calm already fraying nerves, especially when word came through that they would be leaving within a few hours.

They travelled by train to the coast, an agonising journey taking more than two days. They were shunted from one siding to another as more volunteers joined the ranks, or trains with greater priority were allowed to pass through. Late in the afternoon of the second day, the train arrived at a dockside that Arthur assumed – without ever having it proven to him – was Southampton. He boarded a ferry and found himself in the company of men from a number of different regiments: Royal Artillery, Royal Engineers and several regiments of infantry. Arthur, on his own, chatted to many of them, but he never again met any of the men with whom he shared that trip.

On or about 5 June 1940 they disembarked on to a deserted beach at St Valery-en-Caux, 18 miles west of Dieppe, with the guns of battle clearly audible in the distance. The men in his company, without an officer present, waded on to the shore, but once they were there they had no idea what they were supposed to do or to where they were supposed to report. They were finally approached by a sergeant carrying a clipboard under his arm who was attempting to impose some semblance of order.

'Can anyone here ride a motorbike?' he asked, clearly hassled and distraught. When Arthur answered in the affirmative, he got the impression it was the first piece of good news the man had heard for days. With his feet still wet from the water, Arthur was recruited on the spot as a despatch rider.

The bike in question was a 350 cc Ariel with its front headlamp hanging off. The sergeant handed him a despatch and pointed him along the coast road for his destination. When Arthur started the bike up, he found it contained low-grade fuel, had a dirty tank and an almost constantly blocked carburettor. He pushed it as much as he rode it.

The simple system of communicating news of the whereabouts of the 51st Highland Division was a series of despatch riders working in relays along the coast. Consequently, Arthur would ride (or push) the bike along until he met a rider coming the other way. They would trade despatches and turn around. The same system operated right along the two-mile strip of French territory still held by the British. Working his way along the coast, Arthur ran across the battered remnants of the 51st Highland Division, dishevelled, weary and a desperate shadow of the force they had presented on landing. They had been strafed by the Luftwaffe and pummelled by Rommel's 7th Division. Their broken ranks meandered slowly towards the coast in search of some respite.

He was flagged down by one of their officers searching for information, but there was nothing Arthur could tell him; he had no orders regarding their position. The officer was able to tell Arthur that after landing on the French coast they had fought a tenacious and valiant rearguard action for several weeks, but that their days were numbered. Arthur left them as he had found them and thought to himself it was well the people at home were not witness to the scene. They would not have slept soundly in their beds at night.

As the days passed, the sound of shellfire grew closer. It would not be long now before Rommel had forced the British Army into the sea. This totally unequal contest between the exhausted 51st Highland Division and the French 9th Army Corps and the supremely powerful German 7th Panzer Division, the 2nd Motor Division and the 5th and 31st Infantry Divisions, was nearing its inevitable conclusion. The air of inevitable defeat hung heavily over the men, tormented in their retreat by the deadly, terrifying raids of screaming Stukka dive-bombers, unloading their deadly cargoes of anti-personnel bombs. Among the sand dunes of the St Valery beaches, soldiers were maimed or killed by the lateral-exploding shrapnel that whipped across their lines.

As the noise of the bombers faded into the distance, it was replaced by the agonising screams of seriously wounded or dying men. Arthur lost count of the number of times he threw himself from his bike into a ditch as another Stukka bore down on his position. Just when it seemed that they could take no more, the German infantry appeared on the clifftops and began to send down accurate shellfire from their artillery support. When all was lost, the small ships and boats arrived and the men were ordered to swim for their lives. The date was 12 June, more than a week since the beaches of Dunkirk had been cleared.

Understandably, many of the men swam for the nearest boat, but being a strong swimmer, Arthur made for a salvage tug some 500 yards from the beach. He thought there would be less panic further out and less chance of the boat being hit. He swam through the thick oil covering the sea's surface and when he finally made it to the tug, the tyres around the hull were covered in it. Each time he lifted himself clear of the water, he lost his grip and fell back in. He tried frantically, again and again, but he was never close to pulling himself aboard. Finally, almost passing out with exhaustion, he thought of his mother and prepared to meet his maker.

'Won't be long now, Mum, won't be long now.'

He slipped below the water and truly saw his life passing before him. A myriad of images from his past seemed to flash through his mind: his parents, his sister, the vicar of the Holy Trinity church, Harold Isherwood, Jimmy Caffrey, school mates, the members of the church choir, the man in the fishing tackle shop. As his life ebbed away, he felt himself raised to the surface for what was surely the last time.

And then... and then a new sensation. Suddenly, he was pulled by the hair and raised out of the water. Looking up through oil-filled eyes, he thought he could see a short, stocky man in a woollen hat. The vision seemed ludicrous, but this strange man seemed grimly determined not to lose the precarious purchase he had on Arthur's head. He was unable to lift him on to the boat, but as he hung half in, half out of the water, Arthur felt no pain. He dangled, neither saved nor drowned. Then another face appeared and a strong arm came under his armpit and lifted him up the side of the ship, over the rail and on to the deck. Immediately, he threw up and watched in a daze as his vomit, black from the oil, ran down his legs. Then he passed out.

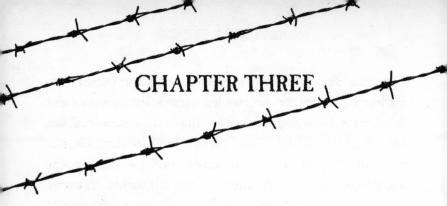

CHAPTER THREE

Arthur landed at Ramsgate and recovered quickly. Apart from swallowing large quantities of oily water, he had not been hurt. He did spend an unpleasant day and a half constantly vomiting, but following a good night's sleep he was really none the worse for his exertions.

After a medical examination, Arthur joined up with a man named Perkins and the pair were sent to Overstrand, near Cromer on the East Anglian coast. There they joined up with a Home Guard unit, drilling with brush handles and manning a Lewis gun without ammunition. Until 1935, the Lewis had been the standard light machine-gun of the British Army, but had since been replaced by the more versatile Bren gun. The Army's surplus guns had been distributed to, among others, the Home Guard. When loaded it was capable of firing 550 .303 bore shots a minute, but in its present state was little more than decoration. The purpose was to give the impression to German surveillance aircraft that Britain was ready and waiting for an invasion but, of course, nothing was further from the truth.

After the miracle of the evacuations, Britain's position in the war did not improve. By the end of June, the Germans were in Paris and the French had thrown in the towel.

Diplomatic relations with Britain were broken off, but the reality was that France had not recovered from the dreadful losses two decades earlier when more than three million Frenchmen were killed on French soil. France was not mentally, economically or militarily ready for another war and Hitler knew it. Though Churchill and his ministers continued to lobby the American government for financial aid and supplies, Britain would have to defend her shores alone.

Arthur and Perkins had only been at Overstrand for a couple of days when the first reconnaissance Heinkel flew over. The German airplane flew down the coast on a level just below the clifftops and was so close that Arthur could clearly see the pilot's grinning face. Arthur was not sure what annoyed him the most, the German's arrogance or his own inability to take a pop at him. As the Heinkel circled around directly overhead, both Arthur and Perkins threw themselves to the ground, memories of St Valery still frighteningly fresh in Arthur's mind. Instead of firing, the pilot gave them a condescending wave and the aircraft disappeared.

Arthur spent only a couple of weeks in East Anglia before he was transferred to Perth, where he became a member of the RASC 'B' Company (Ammunition) and, by coincidence, was attached to the 51st Highland Division. As a driver mechanic, he looked after the division's commandeered lorries, which included Albions, Morris Commercials, Ford Surreys and a Ford Sussex. The division was transferred first to Grandtown-on-Spey, near the naval base at Lossiemouth, and then to Kinbrace, way up in the Sutherland highlands about fifty miles south-west of John O'Groats. There they took delivery of thirty brand new three-ton Bedfords.

Since a great number of the 51st had been killed or captured in France, their numbers had been considerably supplemented by new conscripts, most of whom were Glaswegian lads. For a while, Arthur found them impossible to understand and he became the butt of their humour, which escaped him. Slowly, as he began to interpret their dialect he found them to be a sound and loyal bunch.

He shared a tent with three of them, two of whom were brothers. Charlie and Andy were from the notorious Gorbals district of Glasgow and they each carried bike chains and had razor blades stitched into their coat lapels. Arthur had a Rolls razor, a gift from his sister, which had rusted badly after his dip in the channel.

'Och, mon!' exclaimed Charlie. 'Yiv no need tae poot up with that! Send it tae the makers and tell 'em what happened tae yae.'

He did and a short while later he was rewarded with a brand new model that was the envy of the company. One day the razor disappeared at the same time Andy had gone on leave for the weekend. Charlie followed the next day on a 24 hour pass and came back without Andy, but with the razor. Charlie had found his brother trying to sell the razor in a pub and beat him up. If the retribution was excessive, he nevertheless demonstrated some awareness of the difference between right and wrong.

During August of that year, the nation held its collective breath as the Battle of Britain took place in the sky over Kent.

The newspapers published the daily figures of aircraft being shot down and Arthur felt that even if they were exaggerated, it was obvious the RAF was giving the Luftwaffe a bloody nose. On 15 August alone, the papers reported the loss of nearly two hundred Stukkas. Arthur wondered how many of those Stukka pilots had been responsible for the raids on the stranded troops on the French coast and was satisfied that particular score was being settled. With Goering's Luftwaffe repelled, an invasion had been temporarily averted and both Churchill and the media milked it for all it was worth. But nobody was in any doubt that the war was far from over.

In North Africa, British troops had driven the Italians across the Libyan border and this first major success of the land forces was encouraging after the debacle in France. In the spring of 1941, attention was drawn to events in the Atlantic and the activities of the German battleship *Bismarck*. The HMS *Hood* was sunk and a great sea battle ensued before the *Bismarck* herself was finally sunk.

At the same time, orders were issued for volunteers for Africa, and Arthur was keen to get involved. Initially he was rejected but as the urgency for more men increased, the same medical officer who three weeks earlier failed Arthur, allowed him to go as long as he was not on active service. He was put on board the SS *Duchess of Athol* and set sail from the port of Glasgow's King George V dock. The troops disembarked from the *Duchess* and boarded the *Stratheden* together with wounded Canadian soldiers from the masses already lined up on the quayside. This was one occasion when Lady Luck was smiling on the Cheshire man, prompting him to believe somebody was looking after him. The *Duchess of Athol* taking the remainder of the Canadian wounded was sunk by a U-boat on that transatlantic crossing.

The *Stratheden* headed unescorted to Halifax, Nova Scotia, to deliver the wounded Canadians. Not all of them made it, some of the worst cases being granted a burial at sea, Arthur attending most of the services and Captain French always officiating. When news was received that a U-boat was in the vicinity, the ship's sirens would summon the men to their boat stations and the *Stratheden* would adopt the precautionary zigzag path.

The British soldiers were route marched around Halifax for some much-needed exercise but their reception was not one they cared to remember. Because of the loss of Canadian troops in the war thus far, some people hurled abuse and threw stones at the British lads, who were embarrassed and angry. They were glad to get back on ship. From Halifax they sailed to Cape Town, South Africa, for refuelling before heading to Port Said.

On their arrival, Arthur was encamped at Genifa in Egypt and was a regular visitor to the temporary place of worship erected there in the form of a marquee. One Sunday morning, he was alone with the *padre* at the chapel entrance when they heard the unmistakable noise of a Wellington bomber in trouble. They looked up and watched helplessly as the aircraft circled briefly before dropping out of the sky. They were at the scene of the crash within minutes, but there was nothing to be done. The crew and five passengers were dead and their charred and bloated bodies were laid out alongside the stricken aircraft.

From Genifa, Arthur was moved on to the Base Supply Depot (BSD) at El Kirche and shortly afterwards given orders to relieve the BSD at Tobruk. Due to his experience as a driver–mechanic, normal procedures were overcome in the field and Arthur's captain had his medical status raised to 'A2' (active service) category. Simultaneously, his Colonel ordered him to drive to a recovery shed some distance away to have some damaged cases repaired. When he got back, the men had left for Tobruk, but Arthur was consoled by now being recognised as on active service.

News of the war around the globe filtered through to the men in Africa, the most sensational occurring shortly before Christmas when more than two thousand Americans were killed by Japanese bombers on the Hawaiian US Navy base of Pearl Harbour. The Americans were now in the war and that, at least, was good news. A few months earlier the threat of an imminent invasion of England appeared to have been lifted when Hitler dramatically directed his forces east and invaded the Soviet Union. By September, they had reached Leningrad (St Petersburg) and were laying siege to the city. The following February, Singapore fell and much of the news in the early part of the year centred around the Pacific war between the US and the Japanese.

Back at Genifa, life was pretty good given the circumstances. The men could swim in the 'Blue Lagoon', as the Mediterranean was called, and discipline was relaxed. Watching a new batch of arrivals, Arthur recognised Jack

Hughes, a good friend from Northwich. It felt good to see someone from home. The two men shared a tent and had a lot to talk about. The company was shortly afterwards joined by an arrogant lance-corporal who had those with nothing better to do picking up wastepaper from all corners of the camp. Nobody was sorry to see the back of him when he was transferred.

A few days later, Arthur's company was posted to Ikingee in Egypt where they joined up with 307 Company (Ammunition) and were attached to the 66th RASC, the largest of its kind in Africa. On arrival, almost the first person they came across was the arrogant lance-corporal from Genifa, now wearing his sergeant's stripes.

Once the full complement arrived, the company was moved up to Gambut, near Tobruk, stopping en route at Fort Caputso. They had been allocated 15 old Morris Commercials, but the 30 company drivers were taken in two lorries to the vehicle depot at Mena, where they picked up thirty new three-ton four-wheel-drive Chevrolets on the American lease or lend system. Each truck had two 15-gallon tanks with fifteen two-gallon cans strung on a frame under the baseboard. They were faced with a laborious fuelling operation and straws were drawn to determine the order in which the men would be allocated fuel. Arthur drew the short straw and so was at the end of the queue. While he waited, Jack emptied his allocation into both his and Arthur's two-gallon cans. This meant that when Arthur had finally been supplied, they had the much simpler task of pouring fuel into the larger 15-gallon tanks and a lot of time was saved. The rest of the day was their own and they both set off to see the pyramids.

The following morning, they set off back to Fort Caputso, but after only a couple of miles, Arthur's truck was spluttering and an examination revealed a carburettor full of water. The cans used to fill his tanks had contained water and he was delayed for two days while it was drained. They stayed at Fort Caputso for a fortnight and both Arthur and Jack made the most of the time available to have a look around. The area had been the scene of a battle earlier in the war and the two friends rooted among the debris to see what they could find.

They came across a case of two-dozen cans of bully beef, which they buried in case they ever came back that way and were short of food. Arthur found a German Opal half-track and removed the carburettor which he later fitted to the Chevrolet. Although Opal used the same thread as its American counterpart, it had a larger bore and as a consequence Arthur's fuel consumption went from twenty-five miles per gallon to just eight. However, it was probably now the fastest truck in the desert, a fact that would save Arthur's life before he was much older.

CHAPTER FOUR

Moving up towards Tobruk, the role of Arthur's company was to supply ammunition to the tanks of the 7th Armoured Division, under the overall command of General Sir Claude Auchinleck C-in-C Middle East, and now being pushed relentlessly back by Rommel's Afrika Korps. The RASC's day of reckoning came on 29 May 1942, when they were moved up to the battlefield of the totally inappropriately named Knightsbridge.

Much of the battle took place in what could be described as an elongated saucer, its raised edges giving the location the look of a football stadium. The battle Commanders and the men of the RASC were perched on the saucer's rim and watched a one-sided battle unfold beneath them. The six-pound shells of the German Tiger tanks had a greater trajectory than the two-pound shells of the British Matilda, Valentine and Honey tanks and it made grim viewing.

The battle lasted for just two hours and Arthur was near to tears as it came to a bloody climax. Brave men clambered from their machines screaming, their clothes alight; their tanks were no match for those of the enemy. He had seen dozens of US Sherman Grant tanks on view at Mena, but saw only two this day.

During the battle, the British tanks would raise a grey flag when their ammunition was exhausted and quickly retire to as safe a haven as they could find. On seeing the flag, an RASC truck would be ordered in to meet up with it and replenish its supply. Arthur had been in once, and towards the end of the battle, with the British tanks severely depleted in number, his turn came again.

A spent tank was told by a captain of the Royal Artillery to hold its position and not to seek shelter. Three RASC trucks had been despatched back to the depot for more ammunition and Arthur was behind the wheel of one of the only two trucks still loaded. Despite the stricken tank coming under heavy fire, the captain ordered Arthur into the battle. Scared witless, he had no choice but to obey the command.

'Well, Mother,' he said to himself, 'I guess this is active service. Look after me.'

With his foot almost flat to the floor, Arthur's truck roared towards the tank. He pulled up alongside and almost immediately a Tiger shell went directly through his canopy, missing the loaded shells he carried by inches, but reducing the back of the canvassed truck to its skeletal frame.

Moments later, Arthur was surrounded by a scene of absolute chaos and panic. Defeat had been acknowledged and the captain had given the order to abandon the area. Two Indian gun carriages swept passed him, their occupants waving frantically at Arthur to get the hell out of there. The captain disappeared and Arthur, now with a corporal for company, made to follow him.

Suddenly, a Tiger came into view on the left and moved parallel to them, just twenty yards away. As the turret was trained in their direction, Arthur turned sharply to the right and drove for all he was worth. He expected to be blown to pieces at any second, but the 'souped-up' engine saved his life. As the Tiger receded into the distance behind him, Arthur thanked the Lord for Opal carburettors.

His good fortune continued soon afterwards when driving a mere twenty-five yards behind one of the other four vehicles for which he was responsible. One of his colleagues named Fordham, a Londoner, caught a land-mine. The thunderous explosion had a devastating effect. Arthur was first to the cab door and had some trouble forcing it open. The scene meeting his eyes was catastrophic; his friend's stomach blown open in a kaleidoscope of blood and guts with some limbs virtually dismembered.

Darkness descended and the fleeing convoy lost a lot of time as they searched for the road to Fort Caputso. Once found, they were diverted by a Red Caps road block and told to pick up what remained of the South Welsh Borderers and an Indian division on the Axis road. They passed a deserted NAAFI building stocked with cigarettes, drinks and chocolate. Fearing the advancing enemy would capture the supplies, the captain ordered the stores to be loaded on to the trucks. It was a costly mistake.

The weary troops were not picked up until half-past one in the morning and finally they made their way towards safety. An hour later, they were ambushed; the enemy had chosen the site of the attack carefully. As they entered a short horseshoe bend in the road, the attack broke out and it was immediately obvious there was no escape. A flare lit up the area as if it was the middle of the afternoon and the Germans let them have it. Everyone scrambled from the vehicles in an effort to escape. Snatching up his valise, Arthur ran for the scrub and threw himself flat to the floor as tracer fire came ripping towards him. The sand was kicked up inches from his face and he could hear the bullets whistling just above his head. The scrub offered absolutely no protection at all and it was clear to Arthur that he would be killed in a matter of seconds.

Arthur had thought he was about to die once before, when near-drowned off the coast at St Valery, but he had not experienced the sheer, stark terror he felt now. Once again, vivid pictures of his home and family flashed through his mind. Almost ridiculously, he thought of people and events he had not remembered for years. Faces came to him to which he could not put names. He recalled incidents from when he was a young child. Finally, he saw his mother. He would be with her soon.

A few yards away, a British officer led a company from the Indian division into an attack on a machine-gun post. Screaming at them in their own tongue, the officer charged forward and was bravely followed by his men. They were cut down before they had covered twenty yards. Arthur had never before witnessed such foolhardy, insane courage.

Whether or not it was brought about by this act of reckless daring, Arthur would never know, but suddenly there was a lull in the firing. Arthur did not think twice. He scrambled to his feet and ran clear of the road, diving into a slit trench some thirty yards away. He stopped for just a few seconds to catch his breath and calm his nerves before scrambling away and heading for the coast road. He did not slow down to look back. Reaching some rocky outcrops, he began walking in the general direction of Egypt. The first battle of Tobruk was over.

Before long, Arthur came across another stray who had managed to escape from the ambush. Back home, the man had been a marathon runner with the Nottingham Harriers, but he had damaged his foot in escaping and it was all he could do to walk at all. Arthur stayed with him, helping him along, making the best progress they could.

During the day, they sheltered from the sun and from the sight of German convoys and patrols. The valise Arthur had pulled from his van turned out not to be his own but that of the corporal who had jumped aboard. Inside was a Bible which proved to be a precious crutch in the ordeals ahead of him.

They walked every night, on one occasion coming across a band of Bedouins from whom they were able to buy a dozen bantam eggs. After two weeks, they came across the town of Bardiyah, on the border of Egypt, some sixty miles from where they had been ambushed. Despite his training, the runner was suffering badly from foot blisters, but as Arthur was exhausted from helping his friend, he volunteered to take a closer look at the town. He was gone for an age and Arthur was relieved beyond words when, in the early hours of the morning, he finally returned. The town, he said, was crawling with Germans.

When the day broke, they made their way down into a *wadi*, a dried-up stream containing a number of rocks behind which they could take cover. As they approached it, six German soldiers appeared from behind one of the rocks and confronted them with their rifles pointing directly at them. One of them spoke English.

'Good morning, gentlemen,' he said, smiling. 'We have been watching you for some time.'

They were escorted into Bardiyah and placed with thousands of other British POWs already there. Before long, they learned that Tobruk had fallen on 21 June and something like 30,000 Allied troops had been captured. They were made to strip and bathe in the sea and for Arthur, despite the disappointment of being caught, it was the freshest he had felt for some considerable time.

In the water Arthur was approached by a Welsh lad who suggested they escape by swimming out to sea and into the next bay. The task was a daunting one, but Arthur was confident in his ability to swim the distance and readily agreed. They had advanced no more than twenty yards when they came under fire. The bullets came perilously close and they both immediately stood with their arms raised. As they waded back, they were surrounded by a large number of their compatriots so it was impossible for the German guards to identify the two who had made a bid for freedom.

The following day they were taken to As-Sallum, some twenty miles away across the border. They were held in an enormous valley, ideal for the purpose of securing thousands of prisoners. German guns were mounted on the high ground and trained on the captives. It was here they were addressed by Rommel, the 'Desert Fox' himself, standing in the back of his car. He spoke to them in five different languages and was asked by one of the men how many he knew.

'Thirteen,' he replied.

Raising his head, he talked as loudly as he could, addressing as many of those gathered as were close enough to hear him.

'You have battled bravely for your country, gentlemen, but the fight is over for you now. You will be taken to Germany for the duration of the war. Does anybody have any questions?'

'Food!' shouted several dozen of those standing in front of him. The travelling German food kitchens were excellent and the men, as Rommel promised, were well-fed on rice and gherkins. The following day they set out on a 300 mile trek back into Libya to Benghazi, a major port on the Mediterranean's Gulf of Sirte. Most of the men carried their greatcoats, which, if an almost intolerable encumbrance during the scorching heat of the day, were an absolute necessity to keep out the freezing cold of the night.

The long line of Allied prisoners, stretching as far as the eye could see, was an awesome but depressing sight. The passage of humiliation lasted the best part of three weeks and by the time they arrived at Benghazi, a great number of men had collapsed and been left behind in the desert. They entered the town in the middle of a thunderstorm and were bedded down for the night among the gravestones of the town's cemetery.

They stayed at Benghazi for two days, but rather than being despatched to Germany as they had been told, they were handed over to their Axis allies and put aboard ships bound for the Italian port of Brindisi, on the Strait of Otranto on the Adriatic coast. The men, many of whom were suffering from a variety of tropical illnesses including dysentery, were put on to two filthy, grey coasters. Their South African and Indian allies were boarded on to an older and even more dilapidated rusty-coloured ship. They were crammed like sardines and had to urinate where they stood.

Within an hour of departing, there was an almighty explosion and total panic broke out as each man fought to climb the two steel ladders that led from the hold to the deck. Those unfortunate enough to reach the top of the ladders were immediately battered back down into the hold by the rifle-butt of an Italian guard. News passed down that the explosion had been the ship carrying the South Africans and the Indians, hit by torpedo. All hands aboard went down with her and no attempt was made to pick up survivors. Sitting trapped in the bowels of a ship with a deadly submarine in the vicinity was a severe test of already strained nerves, but the danger passed.

Dropping anchor half a mile from the quayside at Brindisi, the men were ferried in flat-bottomed, over-crowded barges into the port. Arthur saw several men being pushed needlessly and cruelly into the sea. The screams of those unable to swim the short distance to the shore were ignored and several men died. Despite the fact that Arthur had now seen action in two theatres of war, this was the first time he had witnessed an example of needless cruelty.

From Brindisi they were transported to Capua, about three hundred miles away, close to the Mediterranean and about twenty miles north of Naples. They slept on wooden bunks covered in bugs and were fed on just a small piece of cheese and a slice of bread each day. After two weeks in Capua, they were moved another hundred miles north to Farasabrina, near Rome. Four thousand POWs were encamped in large marquees, each holding a hundred men. Despite the morale of the British soldiers being very low, they still managed to have some fun each morning at the expense of their Italian guards. When the roll-call was taken, men would hide and then reappear for the recount. Consequently, the guards were never able to count the same number twice and the process took hours.

They were fed on one ladle of soup and occasionally a bun. On the rare occasions they saw Red Cross food parcels, as many as ten men had to share one package. They would then use the boxes to catch sparrows to supplement their meagre diet. Farasabrina was a hard camp and the dire food shortages were not the only evidence of inhumane conditions. One day, Arthur and his three mates were strolling nonchalantly past a tent when suddenly a New Zealand medical officer poked his head out and urgently summoned them to help him. On a makeshift operating table lay Terry Gorman suffering from a boil down his throat. The MO had no anaesthetic or medical instruments. After the patient had been liberally dosed with spirits, two men took a shoulder each and Arthur and the other chap a leg each whilst the 'operation' was carried out. Unbeknownst to Arthur, the

Green Howard survived the crude operation and the war, passing on eventually in 1997.

Corporal Guscot, whom Arthur had known for some time, approached him as someone who could be trusted to take part in an escape bid. The plan allowed for three of the four men involved to escape and cards were drawn to see who would have to stay behind. Arthur drew a two, a low card, and it was he who had to stand down. The three men were hidden in tea-chests brought in with Canadian food parcels and it was Arthur's job to keep a lookout while the three chests were carried off. After the war Arthur met up with one of the escapees in Hastings. 'Ginger', as he knew him, was able to tell him that once clear of the camp, they made their way to a small fishing port close to Rome and posed as fishermen aboard a trawler bound for the Greek islands. From there, home was an easy run and the three were each awarded an Oak Leaf for their endeavours, a medal that Arthur was denied on the draw of a card. His misfortune, though, was to have far greater consequences.

Arthur spent six months at Farasabrina, after which time, in the early part of 1943, the men were split up and sent to different, more permanent camps. Each was asked on an official form to put down their working skills and Arthur had listed 'cat-burglar'. When the groups were made up, he found his sarcasm had landed him with another two dozen jokers who had given the form similar scant respect. They would travel to their new camp, wherever that would be, together.

The first leg of the journey took them to Florence, 150 miles to the north and a stark contrast to Farasabrina. Here the British prisoners were well-regimented and discipline was well-maintained. Morning assemblies passed without incident and it seemed to the arriving 'rebels' that the men here had accepted their fate. They were part of Wavell's original army and had been imprisoned for the best part of two years. Their policy of 'no disruption' appeared to work, as standards of food and hygiene were high for a prison camp. The new arrivals stuck to their principles of 'no cooperation' during their stopover at Florence. For them, the war was not over.

From there they crossed the border into Austria, bound for Innsbruck. The 25 'rebels' were housed in the same rail carriage and an escape plan began to be formulated. The boards of the carriage floor were rotten and easily broken up. The idea was to wait until the train slowed on one of the many uphill sections of the journey and, one by one, drop through the hole and wait for the train to pass over.

The plan was foiled when the men of the next carriage set fire to some straw. On arrival at Innsbruck, the carriages were all searched and the hole discovered. As it happened, it was extremely unlikely the plan would have succeeded. When the men were taken from the train and placed where they could be watched, and beaten, they noted a heavy guard presence on the roof of the train. They would have been easily spotted.

The train left without them and the miscreants were sent to a nearby stone quarry where they suffered a week of hard labour at the hands of the SS. Their penance served, they were put back on to a train and sent on to Lamsdorf, a huge transit camp for POWs. Here new arrivals were deloused and had their heads shaved. They were also photographed and given their POW numbers. For Arthur, that number was 221925, stamped on both halves of a metal disc perforated through the centre.

From here, some were sent to the graphite mines in Austria and others to farms and factories. The troublesome 25 of Arthur's party were sent to a coal-mine in Poznan and as with most units, Arthur's group contained its 'barrack-room lawyer'. It was he who had instigated the ill-fated escape bid from the train and he had kept a low profile since their visit to the quarry. Now he was finding his feet again.

'The Geneva Convention strictly forbids forcing POWs to help the enemy's war effort!' he told them. 'Working in a coal-mine constitutes just that! We will not go down that mine!'

Their refusal to work led to them being severely beaten with rifle-butts and jackboots. It also meant, after being completely starved for 24 hours, another transfer.

In the east, the Germans had lost half a million men in the freezing cold of the Soviet winter and in North Africa the British Eighth Army had taken Tripoli and Tunis. By the beginning of May 1943, the war in North Africa was won. Since the outbreak of war, many things had happened to Arthur to lead him to this moment, but his fate was now sealed. What followed over the next two years would live with him forever. Early one morning, the 'rebels' were once again crammed into a train carriage and taken south. Twenty-four hours later they had travelled 200 miles to a small town 30 miles west of Krakow. Had they been told the name of their destination, it would have meant nothing to them.

The world was still to hear about Auschwitz. For 182469 Private Arthur Dodd RASC, his personal gates to hell were about to open.

CHAPTER FIVE

The central area of Auschwitz KD (Concentration Camp) was divided into three sections. Camp One was the men's prison and contained Jews, Communists and other 'undesirables'. Camp Two, to the east, was called Birkenau, after the preponderance of birch trees in the small village that was flattened by the Germans when the camp was being constructed. This was the women's camp and where the gas chambers and the crematoria were located. Camp Three was the smallest and known as Monowitz, and was where Arthur and the other British POWs were to be interned.

Around this accommodation were thirty-nine labour camps where prisoners would work in a variety of industrial plants, producing arms, machine parts and chemicals, or in the mines, farms and plantations surrounding the camp. In all, the entire complex was spread over an area of some twenty-five square miles and, according to evidence given at the Nuremberg trials, held as many as 140,000 prisoners at any one time. Arthur was put to work constructing the Buna plant for the manufacture of benzene and synthetic rubber. Any thoughts of refusing to work had quickly disappeared. There was nowhere else to go after Auschwitz; if you did not cooperate here, you were shot.

Each building, made of red brick, had its identity number painted on its gable ends and the part of the Buna plant in which Arthur worked was BAU 38. There were 35 storage huts in a compound oddly known as 'Canada', where the clothes and personal belongings Arthur had seen by the rail-side would have been sorted. Nothing was wasted here; clothing, footwear, brushes, combs, suitcases, spectacles, toothbrushes and even false teeth all had their own storage area. Jewish prisoners who arrived with gold fillings had them extracted and added to the countless fortunes of the Nazi regime.

The different camps were each surrounded by a triple row of barbed wire supported by concrete pylons. High voltage electricity flowed through the wire and along its length, and at intervals of about forty yards were towers from which guards manning machine-guns and powerful searchlights would monitor the prisoners below.

Behind these imposing fortifications, leading German industrial companies had built their factories and I. G. Farben, Krupps, Siemens and Schukert were among the well-known names occupying the labour camp areas. Unionwerke, a subsidiary of Krupps, had an explosives factory there. After the war, I. G. Farben & Company were revealed to have been the manufacturer of the Zyclon gas used to exterminate the Jews. The company maintained Zyclon had been produced only as a disinfectant, but it was classified as *geheimmittel* (confidential) and its key elements were chlorine, nitrogen and cyanide. There were, in fact, two types of Zyclon, carried in identical containers: Type A was a disinfectant, but Type B was used in the gas chambers. Particularly distressing for the British prisoners at Auschwitz was to see that many of the boilers in the camp had been provided by Babcock & Wilcox, a UK company.

For Arthur, the going had been very tough since his capture at Bardiyah. On arrival at Auschwitz, they had marched just 200 yards to the warm and pleasant huts of Camp E711 in which they spent their first fortnight. These had been purpose-built, they later discovered, for the Hitler Youth and had given them a totally false impression of what awaited them. When they were first installed in E711, their barrack-room lawyer had taken most of the credit.

'Farming is better than mining,' he had told them, 'it shows it pays to stick up for your rights.'

When they left the camp a fortnight later and encountered the Jewish girl being beaten by the roadside, the sense of foreboding felt by them all was a far more accurate indicator of what was to come. Their lawyer had been quiet since.

On their first day at the Buna factory they had been divided into working groups, each led by a German civilian and escorted by a German guard. Once organised, they were taken to their place of work. All around them there were prisoners in blue and grey overalls bearing the Star of David constructing buildings and being watched over by an abundance of SS guards. Occasionally, the men would see a Jewish prisoner lying dead on the floor. Later, a cart being hauled along by other Jews would pick up the dead and take them away.

What especially chilled Arthur and his friends during these proceedings was the apparent distorted normality of it all.

Nobody fought back or said a word in protest. It seemed the Jewish prisoners were resigned to their fate. Even when they had nothing to lose, they submitted to this barbaric, inhuman treatment.

Arthur's group were taken to a large enclosure alongside a railway line. Inside were housed long bogie-wagons loaded with pipes of varying lengths and diameters. They were put to work unloading the wagons, being told that this enclosure was to be the technical store for most of the equipment to be used in the factory.

It was like a huge ironmonger's shop, containing valves, tools, timber and neatly stacked bags of cement. Arthur passed the day in a trance, carrying out the tasks set him in a robotic silence. He had witnessed much in the past three years, but he was not prepared for the events that now began to unfold before him. Even that very first day at I. G. Farben or 'the factory' as it was more commonly to be known, the many Jews or 'Stripees' as the nickname-loving British were already calling them, collections of skin and bone in filthy striped garb, many in exceedingly advanced stages of malnutrition, rendered the usually vociferous British Tommys silent in disbelief over what they were witnessing. A group of these unfortunates were working in a field near to where Arthur was similarly engaged when, suddenly and without warning, a shout in good English was clearly audible. 'I'm Leon the Londoner, I should be with you lads, I'm British!' One of the stronger built Jews was then badly beaten by the striped kapo in charge; obviously this scourged nation was not allowed to communicate with other workers. Minutes later the Cheshire man Arthur managed to catch the brave Jew's attention and threw him a packet of ten cigarettes that had just arrived that very morning from his stepbrother. The recipient of the valuable trading currency turned out to be Leon Greenman, and he and Doddy were fated not to meet again until the twenty first century, 2001 in fact, at Leon's book launch in Liverpool.

At midday, the POWs were each given a bowl of soup and a small piece of black bread, made from wild chestnuts and sprinkled with what looked and tasted like sawdust. From what the men could see, the Jews appeared to be barely fed at all, to which their emaciated frames testified. Contact between themselves and the Jewish prisoners was not permitted. In the vicinity of Arthur's group they were involved in the building of stores and offices. They could be seen mixing cement, laying bricks and transporting various building materials in wheelbarrows.

Each Jewish gang was watched by one of the Kamaradschafts Polizei, known as a kapo, who would kick and beat the Jews around the head with their truncheons if they were slow in their work and sometimes even if they were not. Other kapos carried whips. Arthur could not comprehend the insanity of the place when he noticed that many of the kapos, largely drawn from the 'criminal elements' (political prisoners and criminals) of the camp, also wore the Star of David. They were, of course, closely monitored and any kapo who would not harass the Jewish prisoners with the enthusiasm and venom of an SS officer would quickly find himself relieved of his position. Seeing one Jew treat another in this way was good sport for the SS.

The working day was finished at five o'clock and the British prisoners were marched back to Camp E711. They each struggled to come to terms with the events of the day and there was little conversation between them. As they lay in their bunks that night, few of them could sleep, the silence broken only by occasional sobbing. The thought occurred to Arthur, even at this very early stage, that he and his friends had to die here. He could not believe that the SS would allow them to live to tell the tale of what they had been witness to. He lay quietly thinking of home and was sure he would never see it again. At that time Arthur and his colleagues could never even have guessed just how meticulous the Germans could be in their plans for the Final Solution.

The SS were obsessed with the economics of the removal of the Jewish face, considering the life of a Jew totally worthless. While I. G. Farben gave the equivalent of ninety pence per worker per day to the SS hierarchy, they in turn set aside only sixpence per day of that paltry amount for keeping each slave alive.

Zyclon B was shown to be the most efficient eliminator of life, both of vermin and Jews, and was first used at Auschwitz on 4 May 1942. The first site chosen for the gas chambers was too exposed to inmates' eyes and a much preferred position was selected in a wooded area, the new killing centre being built around two old peasants' cottages charmingly whitewashed and topped with thatched roofs.

The first of these elimination centres began operation in March 1943, the very month of Arthur Dodd's arrival at Auschwitz. Arthur found out very early on about the gassing from whispered conversations with Jews working near him.

The next area in which the SS looked for improvements in economic efficiency was to shorten the time needed to burn the corpses. To this end, in 1943, technicians from Topf & Sons, the German firm that had manufactured and installed the furnaces, measured the combustibility of different types of coke and corpses. They concluded that the best oven had consisted of one well-nourished, fast burning adult, one child and one emaciated adult already reduced to skin and bone by starvation and labour. This combination of bodies, once it caught fire, would continue to burn without requiring further amounts of precious coke.

SS Sergeant-Major Otto Moll, overseer of all the crematoria, relentlessly pursued his own fanatically gruesome economics. In new crematorium pits he had slave labourers digging out drainage channels that were sloped so that the fat from burning bodies would run down and collect in pans. That fat could then be poured back on to the fire to make it burn faster, and again save the Third Reich from using their precious coke supplies.

The next two weeks passed in much the same way. Although they watched daily the treatment of the Jews, the only physical injuries incurred by the British prisoners were fractured bones due to a serious calcium deficiency in their diet. From the second day, the good food at the hut stopped and they received little more than potato soup and black bread. They were, to some degree, consoled by the adequacy of their accommodation, but at the beginning of the third week, they were moved.

Their new home was at Camp E715 in the section known as Monowitz, much closer to the synthetic rubber plant and previously occupied by Russian prisoners. These had been worked to death except for the last resilient eighty-odd who were gassed to make way for the more technically competent British POWs. This information had been obtained from a Polish inmate who told them how he had watched as the remaining Russians had been driven like cattle into one of the underground air-raid shelters. The downward-sloping ramps had been closed off at either end with steel doors bolted from the outside. The air vents were then fed with Zyclon B tablets, as were used in the gas chambers in Birkenau, and the accommodation problem was solved.

The senior Wehrmacht officer on the Monowitz site was Feldwebel Messer, the equivalent in rank to a sergeant-major. He was, as were all the German officers, a meticulously smart man in his thirties and, from Arthur's experience, fair and even-handed. When they were transferred to his charge, he took the opportunity to split up the 25 British troublemakers. The lads, taking consolation wherever and from whatever they could, accepted this as a compliment to their generally uncooperative and disruptive ways. They were each accommodated in 25 different huts and assigned to 25 different working parties.

Even by the almost non-existent standards of hygiene at Auschwitz, Camp E715 was a filthy hole. The solitary latrine was a nine-foot cube dug into the ground right outside Arthur's hut. Across it were wooden planks with circular holes in them, where men could do what they had to do, and around it a sheet of corrugated iron for some degree of privacy. Despite their endeavours to de-bug the huts, they were constantly louse-ridden. Arthur's first meal in the new accommodation was fish that he assumed had once been herring. It stank and he refused to eat it, sure that he would regret it later if he allowed himself just one mouthful. Those who tried it were sick almost immediately. Fortunately, Red Cross food parcels were still getting through to the men and without them not one would have survived for very long.

The Jews were daily being beaten, gassed and cremated. For many of them, death was a merciful relief, but the constant smell of scorched hair and burning flesh was nauseating and one that Arthur and his fellow prisoners were never able to get used to. The huge red-brick chimneys, tapering towards the top, towered over the two-storey buildings and were visible from most parts of the camp. Only a change of wind direction gave them any kind of release from the horrifying smell that was a constant reminder of the atrocities taking place around them. Most Jews were gassed within an hour of arriving at the camp, their ashes dumped in the Vistula river, the largest of the three rivers in the vicinity of the camp.

For a while, Arthur was employed digging ditches and laying pipe for a new synthetic rubber plant. Then he was set to pipe bending with Charlie Piddock, an arc-welder with Metro Vicks before the war. Their gang consisted of two young Polish lads, three Ukrainian female welders in their teens and a Mongolian girl-labourer. One of the Poles was a handsome, decent man by the name of Stacha, but the other was known as a *falsche Deutsche*, or 'phoney German', a nasty type who had sold out to the Germans, acting as a spy and an informer. To some degree, Stacha was tarred with the same brush and so nothing was spoken of in their presence. Both Poles were from the nearby town of Oswiecim and did little work. It was safest to assume they were there to monitor any sabotage attempts by the British POWs.

The German foreman, a workaholic who paid great attention to detail, usually had two Wehrmacht guards in attendance. They spent their day in the cabin at the back of the factory where the group took their midday 'soup'. There were also frequent visits from the SS who would crack their whips against their jackboots and scream at the kapos to extract more work from the Jews. If one did not push hard enough, his armband would be torn from him and he would be sent back to work. Once a man had his kapo status removed, he would be entirely friendless in the camp and few survived long.

Arthur Dodd learnt his pipe bending skills from the diligent German engineering foreman, himself a serving soldier in World War One. The first day Arthur was at his work station totally unsupervised, an incident occurred that truly hammered home the fact that Auschwitz was indeed hell on earth. He saw a single Jew crossing a nearby railway line and, as he stared at the forlorn figure, this member of the world's most oppressed race stumbled to the ground as though he had tripped over some sort of obstruction.

ARTHUR'S STORY

First checking nobody was in the immediate vicinity, he went over to see if he could help in any way. The SS would squeeze no more work out of this emaciated human frame, for the Jew was mercifully dead. Deciding to move the corpse notwithstanding the risk, Arthur picked up the small mound of cloth-covered skin and bone with a quick jerk and nearly swung himself off his feet, so easy were the remains to lift. It was a sickening personal moment for Arthur, feeling as he could every single bone of the man's body. He laid the body down carefully on the floor of a nearby hut, the door of which was left open, very fortunate that no Goons (Nazis) were in sight. Literally having felt the abject misery of his new home, it was the most nauseating experience of his life.

It was impossible for Arthur to begin to calculate how many Jews disappeared, but there were thousands more from all over Eastern Europe arriving every day and they never appeared to swell the population of the camp. The trains pulled in and the chimneys of the crematoria continued to blow their deathly smoke into the sky. For the British observers of this grotesque scenario, they had no need to worry about life or death, or whether they were destined for Heaven or Hell when their time came. Their time was now and they were in Hell already.

CHAPTER SIX

There were two currencies in Auschwitz, the *lager* (camp) mark and a system of bartering, the latter of which was by far the most widely used. Guards and labourers who came into the camp from the town were bribed to bring in commodities otherwise unavailable. Red Cross food parcels, though, were the main source of bartering. The most sought after goods were soap, coffee, cigarettes, chocolate and clothing. It was this system that gave the prisoners something to live for.

Due both to its scarcity and the risk in carrying it, clothing was the most valuable commodity and here the artillerymen and engineers had a distinct advantage. Both received regular supplies from their own associations and Arthur was often envious of the goods they received. Arthur himself only ever received one clothing parcel at Auschwitz, and that was so battered and torn it contained just a shirt, a towel and a sock. Sent by his sister, it did however contain a Peterson pipe with a silver ferrel. Pipe tobacco was impossible to purchase in the camp and in order to derive as much pleasure as he could from it, he would meticulously dry out whatever spent tea leaves he could find.

Some temporary release was offered by alcohol. The only drink available was loosely termed schnapps, but in truth was methanol. It was a lethal concoction and those who resorted to it went crazy before succumbing to a slow and painful death. There were notices all over the camp giving warning of its toxicity, but where there is need there will be trade and some of the hardest men sought solace and a permanent escape in this way.

Arthur earned three *lager* marks a week, but they could buy precious little in the camp and nothing at all outside. The cheap paper bore the legend *lagergeld*, the mandatory eagle symbol and a number indicating its value. From the camp could be bought a grey, sudless soap, dubious-looking cigarettes, ersatz coffee and razor blades. The Germans were curiously keen for the prisoners to shave and Arthur always assumed it was for the purpose of propaganda photographs. Arthur and his friends would shave regularly but refused to have their photograph taken.

Making a stand against the wishes of the German authorities had little effect on anything but the men's morale. A Corporal Jim Purdy was in charge of Arthur's hut and he paid consistent and great attention to the men's state of mind. It affected everybody on the occasions when one of the lads broke down. One of the Welsh Borderers became increasingly unstable and began to bare his chest to the Wehrmacht and SS guards, taunting them as they raised their rifles to him.

'Shoot me!' he used to shout. 'Go on, shoot me!'

The guards got to know him well and he was a regular source of amusement to them. They would push him around with their rifle-butts in the confident and arrogant manner of those convinced of the invincibility of the Third Reich.

Alan Blades was a young lad from East Dereham in Norfolk, tall and slim with stainless steel-rimmed glasses. Unlike the Welshman, Alan mumbled to himself and escaped from the horrors about him into a world of his own. He had been captured at Dunkirk at the beginning of the war and had suffered severe hardship over a prolonged period. More and more, he had withdrawn into himself.

Jim Purdy did everything he could to look after the man's interests. As the officer in charge of a group of men, Jim was not required to work each day and kept Alan on light duties. In this way, he could keep an eye on him during the day and Arthur would do the same at night. Only four per cent absenteeism was allowed at any one time, regardless of the general health of the men, and it spoke volumes for the moral fibre of Alan's comrades that not one soldier voiced a word against the special treatment given him.

Another prisoner of E715, by the name of Clatterbridge, was a tall, agile man, known to his comrades to be a religious maniac. He was a devout follower of God's word, but saw every issue in black and white and consequently argued that every German person – man, woman and child – should be wiped off the face of the earth. He would rant this message in the faces of the guards and he came perilously close on many occasions to being shot dead where he stood.

There were varying degrees of mental instability among the men and it showed itself in different ways. One night, as they were trying to sleep, one man rose from his bunk, left the hut and walked straight over to the wire. He had but one thing on his mind and that was to quietly crawl under the wire and leave. Everyone heard the shouting and the gunshots. When the full story emerged the following morning, it seemed he had given the guards a run for their money. When the shooting started, he had fled to the ablutions block and hidden in its attic. There he stayed until the guards burst through the door and sprayed the ceiling with machine-gun fire. The appearance of blood dripping to the floor let them know they had found their target.

An unexpected source of anxiety and distress often came in the form of letters from home. It was unlikely that wives and girlfriends had any idea of the trouble their missives sometimes caused, but many times they were enough to send a man over the edge. A woman's written words could do more damage than anything encountered at the camp.

There were several illiterate prisoners in Arthur's section and often he would read their mail for them. On one occasion, he was approached by the youngest, waving a recently received and precious letter from home. They retired to a quiet corner of the hut and Arthur slowly read its contents to a man who had married not long before he was called up. At the end of the first paragraph, Arthur stopped abruptly. The man's wife had just given birth, yet her husband had been away for what was now the best part of three years. Arthur had to think quickly. What should he do? He pretended he was struggling with the handwriting when in fact he struggled with the dilemma before him. Should he tell the truth or should he omit the offending news and temporarily spare the man's feelings? Obviously, the poor lad would be able to do nothing but stew in his heartache.

Whether he was right or wrong, Arthur could not decide, but he wanted to be no part of anything the man might do to himself as a consequence of hearing this news. He left out the details of the birth and read the letter through as if everything at home was fine. He handed the letter back.

'Thanks, Arthur,' he said, 'you can read the next one she sends me.'

Arthur doubted if there would be any more.

The British POWs took great risks in getting what scraps of food they could to their fellow prisoners in the Jewish section. However, as the British and American Air Forces began a sustained bombing campaign of German cities, so deliveries of Red Cross food parcels became more scarce and it was all they could do to keep themselves alive. Arthur thought back to the time he had spent at Farasabrina and how they had used boxes to catch sparrows. He put the idea to a few of the lads and they spent the next few days searching for birds to capture. In all that time, they did not see one bird in the vicinity of Auschwitz. Whether it was the smell of burning flesh, the smoke of the crematorium or a natural sixth sense that kept the birds away, Arthur did not know.

Arthur was kept busy with the building of BAU 38, bending pipes and making gaskets and their German foreman was keen to keep them at their work at all times. Although Arthur remained convinced he would never see home again, he continued to look for ways to sabotage German operations whenever he could. He forced stones into pipes, fitted blank flanges, always aware of the need to have eyes in the back of his head. As everyone was on the verge of starvation, one piece of information from an informer might be rewarded by additional rations and it was impossible to know who could be trusted. Arthur saw himself as a doomed man who might, even in the most insignificant way, do something to upset the Nazi war machine before he lost his life. The slightest interference for which he was responsible gave him enormous satisfaction.

Although not all the British soldiers participated in these sabotage activities, a great many indeed did. Once they became aware of the materials that were being produced in the gigantic I. G. Farben complex, many prisoners of war immediately protested and refused to work. They unanimously stated that the Geneva Convention expressly forbade using prisoners of war for the production of war materials. They elected from their number a few representatives who were to present their opinion to Gerhard Ritter, the I. G. Farben works manager. In reply to the petition, the Nazi took out his gun from its holster, laid it on the table and, pointing to it with his finger, said, 'This is my Geneva Convention.' Jim Purdy, Arthur's hut leader, said that any POWs not willing to work would be punished by being deported to camps at coalmines.

The war carried on and it was news of it, from radios in the camp and information passed along by a German Jew, that usually brought the most cheer. The Italians had unconditionally surrendered by the end of September 1943, and the Russians were beginning to squeeze the Germans from the east, retaking Kiev at the start of November. Although it was not revealed to the world until after the war, it was at this time that Heinrich Himmler made his now infamous speech declaring his plan for 'the extermination of the Jews' and 'a never-to-be-written page of glory'.

Arthur had spent the previous Christmas in the relative comfort of Farasabrina, but the festivities in Auschwitz towards the end of 1943 were muted and depressing. For Arthur, his life was over. Only his pride, self-esteem and a bloody-minded determination to hang on kept him going. He was unaware to what extent events around Europe were turning against Hitler and his fanatics. The Allies were pushing back the German war machine, but it would be a long time yet before Arthur would see any light at the end of the darkest of tunnels.

CHAPTER SEVEN

During the bitterly cold weeks of January 1944, Arthur's group was joined by a group of Jews controlled by a particularly vicious kapo, determined not to lose his privileges. They were building an internal wall for the new BAU 38 plant and had set up a cement mixer alongside the fire burning outside. Arthur's attention was attracted by the physical condition of one of the Jewish prisoners. The man sidled over towards the fire to steal a few moments of warmth, only to be chased by the kapo within a minute. Seeing his condition, Arthur thought one good blow from the kapo would probably kill him.

He carried bricks on a hod from the pile outside to the site of the wall inside, staggering under the weight of each load. He wore only a flimsy pair of shoes with the soles dangling off and no socks. Arthur decided to find a pair of socks for the man as soon as he could. He had recently received a small parcel from his step-brother, Franklin, and was able to trade 20 cigarettes for a new pair of woollen socks owned by a soldier of the Royal Engineers. The following day, he concealed the socks inside his jacket and looked for an opportunity to slip them to the man.

He was poised to make his move when, from the corner of his eye, he saw the SS officer he had first encountered beating the Jewish girl a couple of weeks after his arrival. He was the epitome of Teutonic arrogance and strode towards Arthur, cracking his whip against the leather of his boots. Arthur froze. He picked up a pipe and pretended he was checking the angle of the bend. The officer walked past him but continued to watch the area for another ten minutes. Eventually, he left and Arthur was able to pass the socks on. The man smiled warmly at him revealing a mouth of blackened or missing teeth.

The following morning, Arthur noticed the man was not wearing the socks and he quickly rounded on him.

'Where are they?' he demanded, pointing to the man's feet. He could speak no English, but knew well enough what Arthur was talking about. He pointed to his mouth and Arthur understood too. The man had traded the socks for food. Two weeks later, he did not show up for work one morning and Arthur never saw him again. He did not need to ask what had happened.

There was only ever, at the most, four hundred British soldiers in Arthur's part of the camp in Auschwitz at any given time and as the Germans strictly applied the maximum permitted sickness of four per cent, there were never more than sixteen men allowed to be off sick. There were two British medical officers in the camp, Captain Spencer and Captain McFarland, and two orderlies working in the Krankenhaus, or hospital, outside of which there were always long queues of men wishing to be considered as being sick.

Arthur had spent two weeks in the camp hospital having lost his voice and running a temperature. The symptoms were not unlike those for typhus, rampant at Birkenau and in the male sector of the Jewish camp. Arthur was treated by Captain Spencer, Captain McFarland and a German doctor by the name of Schmidt, who drew from him a yellow substance during a very painful lumbar puncture. After further blood tests, Arthur was diagnosed as having pneumonia, and he would never have pulled through without the constant care and attention of Captain Spencer who watched over him, mopping his brow every night for a week.

Among the Polish labourers who lived in Oswiecim and worked each day in the camp were a number of partisans who risked their lives as a matter of course to hinder Nazi operations. Once in your trust, they would die for you, but they took swift retribution against any man or woman who betrayed them. Arthur was approached by one of them, who indicated he had been told Arthur could be trusted. He offered to smuggle in radio parts in exchange for cigarettes and chocolate. Arthur was very interested.

Rumour had been circulating in the camp that the war was turning against Germany, but it was impossible to know what was and was not true. The positive effect that such confirmed news would have on the morale of the prisoners was incalculable. Arthur took the man up on his offer. Two nights later, Arthur received the precious parts and made his way back to the entrance of E715. To his horror, he saw that everyone was being thoroughly searched and among those present was the SS officer he had encountered earlier.

This man had made a point of randomly searching Arthur whenever the opportunity arose, but to date had found nothing.

For Arthur, this sudden decision to search everyone was too much of a coincidence. He wondered if the young Pole had been threatened in a bid to set Arthur up. Perhaps their earlier conversation had been observed by suspicious eyes. Arthur's mind was full of the possibilities, but what really mattered was whether he could avoid the very serious situation he now found himself in. There was nobody he could pass the equipment to and he could not drop it anywhere on the open, barren ground. Instead, he had no choice but to have the incriminating evidence found, much to the smug satisfaction of the SS officer.

He was marched from the camp and through several other compounds by the officer and two SS guards before coming to the road that led to the main entrance to the camp. Arthur walked through that now infamous gate bearing the ominous warning: *ARBEIT MACHT FREI*.

The principle of 'freedom through work' was one close to the Nazi heart. When applied to the hundreds of thousands of Jewish prisoners in Auschwitz, the brutal reality was that death was the only path to freedom. For himself, Arthur had no idea what to expect. He was now squarely in the Jewish quarter of the camp and he knew of no other British soldier who had been to this part before him. Certainly, nobody had lived to tell the tale. He had, though, heard enough rumours of red-hot pokers and the extraction of fingernails to give him cause for the gravest concern.

He was pushed roughly through the doorway of a large room where a senior officer of the SS was seated behind a desk.

'Mr Dodd, is it?' he asked, with excessive politeness and an almost Oxford-English accent. 'Take a seat.'

Arthur's palms were damp with fear as he sat down before this imposing man.

'You will appreciate that we do not have time to waste, so I will come straight to the point. I have just one simple question for you and I require from you one equally simple answer, after which you will be returned to your quarters. Who gave you the wireless parts?'

Arthur hesitated before answering.

'The whole thing was a set-up. You know exactly who gave me the parts.'

Arthur did not feel the indifference he tried to convey. A thin, condescending smile spread across the officer's lips, but Arthur's answer was ignored and the question was repeated. Arthur gave the same reply.

'Please, Mr Dodd, do not underestimate the gravity of this situation. Think very carefully before you answer again. From whom did you receive the wireless parts?'

Arthur looked directly into the man's eyes and was under no illusions. He was in very serious trouble.

'You already know,' he insisted.

The officer's smile disappeared in an instant and he nodded curtly to the guards standing behind Arthur. He was hit across the back of the head by a rifle-butt and sent crashing to the floor. There he was kicked mercilessly by the SS officer and the two guards and although Arthur covered his head and rolled into a ball, he could not escape the blows. There was a momentary pause while he was asked the question again. The same answer brought another flurry of kicks and blows.

Arthur was about to pass out when he was dragged to his feet and taken from the room. Another door was opened and he was thrown into a darkened, windowless cell. He lay on the damp floor, finding breathing both difficult and painful. He had a vague feeling he was not alone in the room, but soon collapsed into a deep yet troubled sleep.

He was awoken by the door being flung open and as he was dragged to his feet he seriously doubted his ability to withstand much more punishment. The light from the doorway revealed his cell mate to be the camp leader, the British officer responsible for the POWs who went by the name of Innes, and whose battered, swollen face made it almost impossible to recognise him. Arthur wondered how long it would be before his own physical condition was the same.

He was marched outside and taken towards the main gate. Looking to one side, he saw three Jewish prisoners still strung up after being hanged from a wooden scaffold. As bad as he felt, this chilling sight shook Arthur to the core. He was pushed forward, but instead of passing under the main gates was led through a different part of the camp. They turned away from the Jewish sector and passed only SS guards and their vicious, snarling dogs. He had no idea where he was being taken as he had never before been through this part of the camp, but he was mightily relieved when he arrived outside his own camp and was deposited among the friendly faces of hut E715.

For whatever reason, the SS had decided they had done enough to him. He was strapped up with an old khaki shirt by an orderly and put to bed. The release of anxiety swept over him and despite the pain in his chest, back and limbs and the intolerable pounding in his head, he knew he was very lucky to be alive. In hindsight, Arthur always wondered why the Nazis spared his life on this occasion but after much reflection on the subject, he reached the conclusion that his I. G. Farben hosts had a high regard for British technical expertise. In essence, the products from the German chemical giant were vital to the war effort.

He did not see Sergeant-Major Innes again. He was told he had been heavily involved with the partisans since his arrival at Auschwitz and that fact had been revealed to the SS by an informer. Such was his condition, he was transferred back to Lamsdorf, but Arthur never found out if he pulled through.

CHAPTER EIGHT

After just two days, Arthur was off the sick list and back at work. The food rations did not improve and had in fact continued to worsen, as the effect of Allied bombing cut deep into the German economy. However badly they fared, though, they knew they were much better off than their fellow prisoners in the Jewish sector. Frequently, British POWs would place scraps of food in a variety of hiding places for the Jews to take. This was not done by all. It was the view of more than one POW that it mattered little if a Jew died on a Tuesday or a Wednesday; they would die sooner or later anyway, so what was the point of prolonging their agony? The activity was also punishable with the kind of battering Arthur had suffered and many were not prepared to take the risk. It was a matter between a man and his conscience, but Arthur chose to do what he could.

He had made a friend of a Polish worker by the name of Maria Kostka, who would give him whatever news of the war she was able to pick up. It was from Maria he learned that by the end of January 1944 the RAF were bombing Berlin. She would pass the bulletins on scraps of paper and Arthur would later read them to his comrades eager for news. Maria was 25 years old, born and raised in Oswiecim and a proud Pole who hated the German invaders with an intense loathing.

Early that year, they heard the first of the bombers. From reconnaissance, they had obviously learned of the industry in the area and had started to bomb sections of the camp, some way from where Arthur was. During the attacks, they would be moved to the air-raid shelters and Maria would sing for their entertainment. She had a beautiful voice and would sing the romantic ballads of her homeland from the days when they were free. She often sang with tears running down her cheeks and although Arthur could not understand the lyrics, there was no need. Their passion, warmth and beauty were all too apparent.

Other girls mingled with the British POWs and it was not unusual for romance to blossom. The degree to which this was permitted was entirely dependent on the attitude of the foreman and some decided to turn a blind eye. One soldier from Essex, known as 'Little Darkie', was one of the few POWs at the camp who was younger than Arthur. He became attached to a Ukrainian girl named Natasha, a welder with striking good looks. Such was their mutual devotion to each other, they had decided they would marry and move to England together.

Arthur too was subject to the forces that push people together in such adverse circumstances and he and Maria would snatch whatever moments they could together. One of Maria's responsibilities was to furnish Arthur's gang with the flanges they required and she would deliberately give them insufficient for their needs to have reason to call on

Arthur more frequently. He, in turn, would keep a close eye on the level of the stock and was always the first to suggest their being replenished.

Sunday was generally a rest day and spent away from the overbearing misery constantly endured by their ill-fated Jewish neighbours. There were, though, irritants still to suffer and frequently they came from the French POWs walking Polish and Ukrainian girls on the road outside the Monowitz wire. The British prisoners in the main had refused to sign a parole form that promised they would not attempt to escape if allowed unguarded outside the camp. The punishment for abuse of such a privilege was so severe that few used this form of parole as a means of escape. Some of the French prisoners had no problems signing the declaration and were thus rewarded with a greater degree of freedom. As they passed the British wire, they would taunt and tease the inmates, giving cause to a great deal of anger and frustration.

One Sunday, when standing close to the wire, Arthur and a few of his fellow comrades heard the sound of an approaching motor calvacade and were soon passed by a number of cars containing senior SS officers and, although he could hardly believe it, the head of the Gestapo himself, Heinrich Himmler. Arthur felt his blood chill as he watched the architect of the Final Solution pass by.

The building work went on and Arthur was involved with a project of installing boilers which required the erection of scaffolding. A lad from the Royal Engineers known as 'Big Darkie' had earned some respect in the camp for the brilliance with which he could move thirty-ton boilers around using only a winch and wooden rollers. With the assistance of only two sixty-year-old Polish labourers, they moved the boilers over ditches and around corners, patiently moving them, foot by foot, towards their objective. It was an amazing sight to behold. He had, before the war, been an employee of Babcock & Wilcox, so if his surroundings were unfamiliar to him, the boilers were most certainly not. With his quite brilliant mechanical mind, he became totally absorbed by the challenges set him and he seemed better able to cope with the tapestry of horrors offered by Auschwitz.

Working alongside Arthur was a chirpy little Scouser by the name of Shaw, a former lorry driver for Pierrepoint. They got on well together and exchanged many stories about their experience and knowledge of HGVs. Big Darkie had ensured that the installing of the boilers had been completed without problem and Arthur and Shaw were employed to dismantle the 150-foot derrick erected for the purpose. They proceeded in a slow, methodical way to bring it down, but were constantly harried by the German foreman who saw their pedantic labours as a less than subtle form of time wasting. He cut corners, saved time and ignored warnings that the whole structure was in danger of coming down a lot more quickly than he intended.

Inevitably, the derrick came crashing down, and did so with fatal consequences. The main part of the structure fell on to the roof of an electrics workshop and killed 20 Jews working inside almost instantly. The deaths mattered little to the hierarchy of both the SS and the directors of I. G. Farben & Company, but the loss of the premises was taken very seriously indeed.

Arthur and Shaw ran into what was left of the building to offer what comfort and assistance they could to the wounded, but there was little that could be done. No British soldiers were normally allowed into the workshop and Arthur could see why. It was a huge complex with rows of electric motors and a multitude of plinths on to which more electrical equipment was being lowered. This was probably the nerve centre for the entire camp.

The foreman was led away to be transferred, no doubt, to the Russian front. The SS showed no mercy to those who failed, even their own. A man who was guilty of working too feverishly in the cause of the German war effort was to be rewarded with a sentence that was almost the same as the death penalty.

As 1944 wore on, the British POWs became practically anaesthetised to the brutal treatment of the Jews. The officers of the SS seldom thought a Jew was worth the cost of a bullet, it being commonplace to see the most severe beatings taking place or a man near death through exhaustion having the last remnants of life smashed out of him. A man would be kicked until the last twitches and nervous spasms stopped. Those witness to this daily horror had each to handle it in their own way, but they were all deeply traumatised to varying degrees. One man who arrived with black hair saw it turn grey within a week.

There was no such thing as a good night's sleep. The noises of deeply troubled men crying and shouting out throughout the night made it difficult to put together more than a couple of hours of unconsciousness. Even when total exhaustion brought some temporary relief, it was usually accompanied by horrific, distorted nightmares.

'We don't sleep,' noted one demoralised observer. 'We just take it in turns to keep everyone else awake.'

In addition they might be woken at any time and tossed from their bunks. The cause might be a spot-search or, more frequently, entertainment for bored SS guards. It had the effect of maintaining a state of high tension. Men could never relax, tormented by their own thoughts and the menacing presence of sadistic guards. Many of them just went mad, snapped away from reality into a world even more dreadful than the one they had left. Some took to methanol as a form of suicide.

Each morning at five o'clock, the men would be woken by the macabre sound of the Jewish orchestra playing at the main entrance as the new arrivals were being sorted into two groups. One group would be put to work; the other would go straight to the gas chambers. At six o'clock, the door of the hut would be kicked open by one of the Wehrmacht guards amid the same routine of shouts and threats each day.

'Heraus! Schnell! Sie arbeiten schwer heute!'

With the shouts would come the dreadful smell of the crematoria with which they lived every waking moment. There was no breakfast, just shouting, prodding and bullying in preparation for the six-thirty departure to the factory. The men were constantly weak and hungry, their bones protruding grotesquely through a thin, pale skin. Their heads ached almost permanently and their limbs were sore with beatings and malnutrition. Heavy with despair, there was precious little to live for. Arthur had no dreams of ever going home; they will not, he thought repeatedly, let us live to tell this tale.

On the short walk to the workplace, they would pass any number of Jewish corpses, beaten to death where they had fallen. They would witness many of the beatings, but knew now the price of interference was death. Once at work, they were never out of earshot of men and women screaming. It was a constant torment in the background.

Watching these people, Arthur became able to judge fairly accurately how much life was left in a man, although he was occasionally surprised at the determination of some to stay alive. The four-wheeled high-sided carts were pushed around the camp by two or three Jews who would stop to pick up the bodies of those recently shot or bludgeoned to death. It took two of them to pick these skeletal frames as the men on the carts were only days away from death themselves.

The scene surrounding Arthur Dodd was one of constant horror, depravation, misery and despair. As the winter began to ease and spring of 1944 approached, there was no comfort for him. With the warmer weather would come disease and an increase in the stench of rotting flesh that was almost beyond human endurance. In private moments, he felt it was impossible to feel more thoroughly desperate, more utterly unhappy and more painfully miserable.

But it was a long way from being over.

CHAPTER NINE

Slave labour was very much a part of the workforce at the Buna plant: Russians, Ukrainians, German Communists, gypsies and, of course, Jews from all over Europe were pressed into service in the cause of the Third Reich. In the course of his own forced labour, Arthur saw men and women from a variety of nationalities and social backgrounds.

Arthur spent most of his time pipe bending on a large wooden table with a metal worktop. Moveable steel pegs were secured in holes and traced the degree of bending required. Each pipe was filled with sand to avoid splitting. Once at their workplace, they would work all morning until 12 o'clock, at which time they would be fed a serving of what was referred to as 'dishwater' soup. A 20-gallon container was deemed sufficient to feed the several hundred people working in this part of BAU 38. The POWs were always fed first and what scraps remained were fed to the Jews.

The British POWs often got into arguments with the guards of both the Wehrmacht and the SS. They would frequently hurl abuse when a Jew was subjected to a beating and even if they had learned how far they could go, they did not let incidents of brutality pass without comment. Whenever the dissent became excessive, a guard would slip his revolver from his holster or raise his rifle and the objectors would generally stand down.

The working day would finish at five o'clock when they were returned to their respective huts. They were occasionally searched when entering the compound, as Arthur had been when carrying the wireless parts, but the men had no idea when it might happen. They might be stopped on three consecutive nights and then not be searched again for a fortnight. There was no way of knowing.

At half-past six, they would form a queue outside the hut to take their share of the bread and soup left for them. Jim Purdy would make sure the meagre rations were shared out fairly. Occasionally, perhaps once a fortnight, Jim would hand out the mail that had arrived and the men would form a separate queue in hope more than expectation of good news from home.

Lights went out at precisely ten o'clock each night and before then Arthur would spend those hours he had to himself reading the King James Bible he had picked up at Tobruk. The print was extremely small, but Arthur would study it carefully each evening, to maintain his faith and his spirit. Each of the prisoners was issued with one of the gospels from the New Testament, but few bothered to pray in such a god-forsaken place. Arthur himself could not have coped without prayer and took his small Bible with him everywhere in his field-dressing pocket.

When the weather was good, Arthur would step outside and stroll along the wire with the other lads. In this way, men from different huts met up and pieces of news and gossip were exchanged. There was also some banter about their respective areas of the country and their football teams. Light-hearted moments, though, were rare.

Sabotage was a thriving activity and the men would trade stories about what they had been up to. Filling pipes with rubble and loosening nuts after work had been inspected and passed was a regular trick. The men deliberately miscounted when mixing concrete and ensured the mix was too heavy with cement causing cracks in the structures that were built. One Polish electrician connected the mains to the water supply and then quickly disappeared. Another man obtained a whistle and caused umpteen delays in the working day by blowing it when he was out of sight. In these ways, the men did what they could to ensure that what could go wrong, did go wrong.

The prisoners were constantly subject to abuse and tensions ran high. On one occasion, an SS guard burst into the technical *lager* and beat up a Jewish prisoner. After kicking and punching him repeatedly, he sent him sprawling into a British POW. The soldier snapped and stormed over to the guard and put a fist up to his face.

'You square-headed bastard!' he screamed, spitting in his face as he spoke. The guard went to draw his gun, but other lads standing by walked across and put themselves between the man and the guard. Anything could have happened, but finally the guard returned the gun to its holster and walked away.

Such incidents sometimes ended with a sickening incident. A group of POWs marching to work passed a young girl struggling with a dixie of soup. One of the lads, Private Campbell, took it from her to ease her burden, but was almost immediately tapped on the shoulder by an SS guard and told to pass it back. The soldier refused and stood his ground. Without hesitation, the guard ran him through with his bayonet and the man appeared dead before he hit the floor, but did, in fact, survive. It was never possible to know how far an SS guard could be pushed.

On another occasion in the kitchens, a young Jewish boy picked up a piece of potato peel off the floor and ate it. He was spotted by a Polish woman, a *falsche Deutsche*, who knocked him to the floor. She then proceeded to throw at him whatever came to hand and was only prevented from killing him where he lay by the intervention of a handful of British POWs.

Generally, the POWs would help when they could, but most of the time there was little they could do to intervene. One of the lads was approached by a young Jewish boy and asked for a 'piece' of a cigarette. When cheerfully told he was too young to smoke, the boy explained that it was for his father, who was a surgeon, and his older brother to share. When asked about his excellent command of the English language, the soldier was told that before the war the boy would spend six months of the year in Cromer, near Great Yarmouth. The soldier gave him his last full cigarette.

Two POWs once went into the factory kitchens to collect soup and bribed one of the kitchen hands to insert a figure '1' before the '25' rations written on the order sheet. The ten Jews working alongside them that day devoured the surplus rations. A POW escaped a severe beating once by quickly mingling with other prisoners after standing up to the guards. Later, he was passed a note by a young Ukrainian girl who had admired his courage. He had the note translated: 'Be careful. Do not become a flower in Auschwitz.'

Near the entrance to the gas chambers were enormous beds of flowers and it had become symbolic for many Jews to pick a flower and take it with them to their death. The story was well-known in the camp and the girl's message was not lost on the man. On another poignant occasion, a truck full of Jewish women arrived. From the picture of health they presented, it was clear that they had only recently been arrested and the POWs attention was drawn to them as they sang together in Yiddish with voices so beautiful barely a word was spoken by the men watching. They were beautiful and brave and Arthur had to fight back the tears. They had voices like angels, he thought, being driven to Hell.

Despite the treatment being handed out by the guards, especially those in the SS, not all the Germans in the camp were the same. One particular Wehrmacht supervisor was respected by the POWs. He was older than most of the other guards and treated the men with the respect he felt they deserved as fellow soldiers. He was once leaving the camp to go home to Cologne on leave and was presented with a package by the men. Knowing how hard times were for ordinary Germans, they had presented him with two packets of cigarettes, two bars of chocolate and a block of soap. Aware of how much they needed these rations for themselves, the man was overcome and cried in front of them.

In the July of 1944, rumours were rife that someone had attempted to assassinate Adolf Hitler. At first, the stories suggested he might be dead, but before long the word went around that he was not even seriously injured. In the August, there was a new arrival at Auschwitz, but it was many years later before Arthur ever heard of her. In Amsterdam, the Frank family were arrested by the Gestapo after spending two years in hiding in the attic of their home. Among those sent to the camp was Otto Frank's daughter, Anne. Her diary was to be a potent testimony against the anti-Semitic regime of Germany's fascists long after her death.

As the summer drew to a close, the Germans were on the back foot. The Normandy landings had given the Allies a vital foothold on the continent and Paris was recovered by the end of August. Arthur did not know it, but the beginning of the end had arrived.

CHAPTER TEN

A round this time, a soldier nicknamed 'Taffy the Choir' got to work on the vocal cords of his fellow prisoners and his exacting demands produced a splendid oral performance at the carol concert. Such moments heavily reminded Arthur of the Holy Trinity church back at home in Castle.

Sergeant-Major Innes, the commanding POW officer badly beaten by the SS and returned to Lamsdorf, had been replaced by Sergeant-Major Charlie Coward from the Royal Artillery. He was a native of Edmonton, north London, and had been taken prisoner at Calais in 1940. A large number of POWs arrived with him and assuming control he called a meeting of hut leaders, which included Jim Purdy. Jim passed on to the lads Coward's sentiments that the men at the camp appeared to him to resemble zombies more than soldiers.

'Wait until he's been here a few days,' one said, 'and see what he has to say then.'

The Commonwealth was well-represented at the meeting by George Randall from Cape Town and Ted Cockerell from Australia. Coward's attitude was to give the Germans the appearance that all was as it should be, yet to pursue a strategy of continuous sabotage. Every opportunity to inhibit the German war machine should be taken.

The subject of informers was brought up and a man from Durham by the name of Miller, who served with the Green Howards, was mentioned. Apparently, he had arrived alone at the camp from Lamsdorf three weeks earlier and had aroused suspicion. Coward told the men not to discuss anything in his presence and ordered the only two other Green Howards in the camp to keep a watch on him.

At this time, Coward was able to communicate with officers at Lamsdorf and he sent a message requesting details on Miller. In the meantime, the other two Green Howards casually questioned him on regimental details, such as officers' names and troop movements and he seemed very reluctant to answer their questions. Finally, word came back that nobody by the name of Miller with the Green Howards had come from Lamsdorf to Auschwitz.

The following morning, a handful of men followed Miller into the latrines and killed him. He disappeared into the pit. It did not surprise anyone that no comment was made by the Germans about his sudden and permanent absence. It did surprise some though, that the usually meticulous Germans had decided to place Miller in the Green Howards Regiment, one of the smallest and thus one of the easiest for them to check out.

Lance-Corporal Reynolds was a gentle man from the Midlands who was popular with the other men. On one freezing morning, he was ordered by an arrogant Unteroffizier of the SS to climb a recently erected steel pylon without rubber boots, climbing kit or gloves. Reynolds refused on the reasonable grounds of safety, but as he walked away towards the other lads, the German officer drew his pistol. The lads shouted a warning, but as Reynolds turned he was shot in the chest and killed instantly.

Two days later, Coward led the entourage to a nearby cemetery where Reynolds was buried with a Union Jack flag draped over his coffin and as much military honour as the men could muster. The occasion was one of quiet dignity and respect, but it was little consolation to the men that the SS officer was removed from the camp and not seen again. Arthur had been a good friend to the man and hoped with all his heart that the murderer was on his way to the Eastern Front.

About this time, at the start of October 1944, Arthur was approached by the same Polish worker who had arranged for him to receive the wireless parts. He told Arthur that the local partisans were in need of the assistance of a few British POWs who could be trusted. They knew from the wireless incident that Arthur was such a man. The feeling of trust, however, was not entirely mutual. Arthur still had the bitter taste in his mouth of the beating he had received and was not satisfied the Pole was not responsible. On the other hand, Arthur did not expect to survive Auschwitz and he was always tempted by any chance given him to put one over his captors. He had heard of the activities of the partisans, which included the regular assassination of German officers in the nearby town of Gleiwitz and decided he would go along with him. A couple of days later, he met up with the Pole and told him he had decided to help.

At about half-past four that day, Arthur was alone in the factory checking some pipe bends when he was approached by his contact and taken to the far end of the building, the first time he had been in that area. There were a number of bays filled with ceramic filters and after nervously checking that they were not being watched, the Pole began to claw out a hole behind one of the smallest of the filters. Having done so, he told Arthur to climb in and wait for someone to collect him. This he did, but it was extremely cramped and uncomfortable.

Before long, Arthur heard the other prisoners leaving the factory and being assembled outside. He assumed the Pole would make sure the head-count was OK. Inside the filter bay, Arthur was terrified and had no idea what he had let himself in for or what would happen next. He did not know if he might be given the opportunity to escape or even if he might have been lured into a trap.

After an hour, he could bear it no longer and worked his way out of the mountain of filters and stood alongside his hiding place in the now deserted factory. He could hear the sound of dogs barking in the distance, but little else. He stood there for hours, not knowing what or for whom he was waiting. His nerves were getting the better of him when he heard a muffled sound from the shadows.

Frightened half to death, he was beckoned by a nod of the head to follow as a man left the factory. As they made their way across the open ground, they had to keep an eye on the sweeping searchlights and take cover as they came around. His escort was another Pole, but he spoke no English and told him with sign language to stay tucked in behind him. They made their way under the wire of Monowitz at a point already prepared, then crossed over a road and some scrubland. After an hour, Arthur had no idea where he was, but felt certain they were well clear of the huge Auschwitz complex. Any sense of freedom, though, was crushed by fear and anxiety.

Coming across another road, they were met by an old wagon and climbing on to the back, he found himself to be one of five British POWs that had broken out of the camp. There was a tall Guardsman he knew as Ginger, two Geordies and a Yorkshire lad nicknamed 'Halifax'. After a short journey in the wagon, they were dropped at a small copse and were approached by the local partisan leader who introduced himself as Alex.

Alex was a huge, burly man, clad in a sheepskin jacket and a bobble hat. His English was poor, but he was the only one they could talk to as the other four Poles spoke no English at all. He explained to them that they had learned of the importance of the electrical installation since the derrick had collapsed into it. It was their intention to blow it up and Arthur and his four comrades were required to help carry the explosives to the camp.

They were given a lift part of the way back, but again had to walk for the best part of an hour to complete the journey back to I. G. Farben. They carried boxes of explosives, batteries, sticks of gelignite and rolls of wire. They then re-entered the camp the same way Arthur had left it. The five POWs watched as the Poles wired up the electrical installation and then helped them as they trailed the wire back to the fence. Once a safe distance away, the detonator was plunged.

The explosion was muffled, but they saw and heard enough to know that considerable damage had been done. Wasting no time, the ten men quickly distanced themselves from the camp and Arthur felt a sense of elation he had not felt for some considerable time.

Back at the copse, Alex would not allow a fire to be lit for fear of giving away their position, so they had to eat raw meat. Arthur was only able to chew it for so long before spitting it out, but it was still the best thing he had tasted in an age. With the meat, they had white bread, wine and genuine local schnapps. The POWs talked among themselves, high on the adrenaline of the mission and their escape from the camp.

They were surprised and somewhat alarmed when Alex later announced that they would be going back to I. G. Farben the next night to lay more explosives at the electrical installation. Although it had been badly damaged, it had not been destroyed. The five British lads thought such a mission was suicide and said so. They were convinced the factory would be swarming with guards as a consequence of their success.

They took what sleep they could and spent most of the next day laid up in the copse like frightened rabbits. The food was the same as the previous evening except in daylight it looked slightly less appealing. The Poles chatted in their own tongue, but Arthur and his mates were tense and quiet in fear of what the coming night would bring.

Alex was aware of their mood and knew too that now outside the camp they were keen to make good their escape and get well clear of it. When they approached him on the subject, he told them of the importance of completely destroying the installation, but that after the job was done, he would give them whatever help he could in getting away.

On their way back to the camp that night, laden again with wire and explosives, Arthur was convinced that he would either be killed in the next few hours or captured and beaten to within an inch of his life. Very few words were spoken on the journey. As it turned out, the mission was as successful as the previous night and Arthur was astonished at there being no reception committee waiting for them. Once they were safely back at their makeshift camp, Arthur and the other lads once again brought up with Alex the matter of their escape. They were less than impressed with Alex's answer.

'Gentlemen, very rare I have ten good men to do work. We must do as much damage as we can. One more task. Then you go. I help you.'

They had no choice but to follow his wishes. It would be pointless attempting the arduous journey before them without a great deal of assistance from the partisans. They were also acutely aware that this was war, they were soldiers and Alex was fighting the same enemy, taking no less risk himself than he was asking them to take.

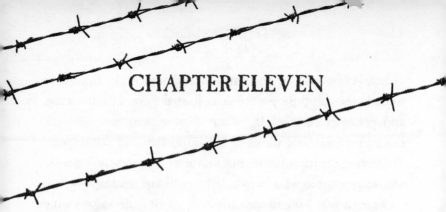

CHAPTER ELEVEN

On the third night, they were loaded up again and set off with their Polish comrades, who they now trusted implicitly. They were by this time familiar with the local terrain and before long Arthur realised they were heading back to the factory. He could not believe they were going to the installation for a third consecutive night. The men exchanged furtive glances, each thinking the same thing.

Once more, they scrambled under the wire, laid the charges and retired some distance away. Again they were unchallenged. Arthur had nothing but admiration for these Polish partisans and accepted now that they knew exactly what they were doing. By the time they left I. G. Farben that night, they had not only destroyed what was left of the installation, they had also effectively sabotaged the preparations the Germans had made in the past 48 hours to rebuild it. The site was so badly damaged, it would be difficult to build anything there for some time.

On their return, Alex again told them that they must do 'one more job', but there were strong indications this time that he meant it. He handed one of the Geordies a rough map of the area, pointing out certain landmarks.

'You will escape tomorrow,' he told them.

'We can't be going to the installation again,' Arthur said, 'there's nothing left of it.'

Alex smiled. 'No, we are finished there.'

They were prepared to believe him. On the fourth day, there was added tension with the realisation that they would be on their way within a few hours. There being no light in the evenings, Arthur had changed his routine and read his Bible during the day. He found it difficult, however, to concentrate. He prayed for peace and an end to the war, and he prayed for the tormented Jewish people inside the camp, but his adrenaline was running high and it was difficult for him to think of much else but their forthcoming bid for freedom.

Before they left the camp, Alex embraced each of them in turn and shook their hands. What he said reassured them that he was as good as his word.

'We will not see each other again after this night,' he said, 'and we may not have the chance to say farewell later. Thank you for what you do for my country. Good luck.' Even the Poles who were travelling with them that night shook hands with them. There might not be an opportunity later. They were unable to understand each other's words, but translation was unnecessary.

They left the copse and travelled back towards Auschwitz, this time moving further to the east of Monowitz. The British lads were not sorry to see this, believing they had well and truly exhausted their good fortune in the other direction. As they neared the camp, it was clear they were approaching one of the Jewish sectors and Arthur was reminded of a rumour he had heard some time earlier of a planned mass break-out. Perhaps their mission this night was to coincide with that. This possibility was reinforced by the equipment they took with them. There were no explosives. Indeed, the British members of the party were not required to carry anything, but among the tools carried by the Poles were, Arthur suspected, wirecutters. As they approached the camp, it was eerily quiet except for the sound of barking dogs in the distance.

Then suddenly, when they were still some hundred yards from the wire, powerful searchlights were switched on, blinding the men and lighting up the area as if it were mid-afternoon. Within seconds, a blanket of machine-gun and rifle fire opened up on them. After being momentarily stunned, they ran for cover as quickly as they could. Arthur expected at any second to feel the piercing pain of being shot in the back. Alongside him were the two Geordies. As they ran they each in turn stumbled and fell before scrambling back to their feet and carrying on. Arthur felt again that his life was about to end, but this time there were no images of home and loved ones. Without any thought for his injured foot, he ran for his life as hard as he could. Dr Booth would have been impressed.

After a couple of minutes, the machine-gun fire receded behind them and they fell to the ground exhausted, barely able to breathe. Arthur, with the two Geordies, had become separated from the rest of the party and, looking around in the darkness, had no idea where they were. For a few minutes, the three men were totally unable to speak.

On reflection, they agreed that the gunfire had not been aimed at them. They were easy targets, but to their knowledge nobody had been hit. It seemed far more likely that the Germans had been informed of the break-out and switched on the lights as the Jewish prisoners were to meet up with the partisans. In the bedlam that followed, they had been able to escape and had possibly not even been seen.

They waited for the Poles, Ginger and the Yorkshire lad to appear and they searched their immediate area carefully. They could find no sign of them. They were on their own. Arthur thought through what had happened on the previous nights and it was obvious that the plan to destroy the electrical installation was part of a plan to reduce the amount of lighting available to the Germans at the time of the break-out. In this, they had failed. The Germans had either utilised an installation in another part of the camp or had not been dependent on it for security lighting in the first place.

Although Arthur was not aware of it, the events at the camp that night marked the only occasion when a considerable number of Jewish prisoners reacted against the regime at Auschwitz. Some 860 Jews, generally those with professional skills, were put to work in the area of the gas chambers and the crematoria. Collectively known as a Sonderkommando (Special Command), their duties included the gruesome task of disposing of the bodies of fellow Jews. It was the most degrading and awful work that took place in the camp, but for the short time they were allocated to it, they were given some degree of preferential treatment. They were generally not badly beaten and their rations were sufficient to sustain them. After four months, to reduce the risk of news of what was going on at Auschwitz ever reaching the outside world, the entire Sonderkommando was exterminated and replaced. Many observers have noted how little the Jews resisted the oppression of the Nazi regime, but this particular group of men decided they would not go quietly to the ovens. Using weapons provided by the local partisans, they planned to shoot their way out of the camp. In this they failed miserably, but not before 70 officers and guards of the SS had been killed. Not one member of that Sonderkommando survived the day, but they did at least go to their deaths with their dignity restored.

The three British POWs decided to set off, but they had no idea where they were and so no idea which way to go. They had the rough map given to one of the Geordies by Alex, but it was impossible to fix on any landmarks in the dark. Their priority, though, was to distance themselves from the camp and they put several miles behind them by dawn. As day broke, they slipped into a roadside ditch and discussed what they should do next. They decided they would walk in the night and rest during the day. Their next problem was hunger and they thought the only realistic prospect of finding food was to forage in the smallholdings of local farms and look for vegetables.

They made good progress on the second night and in the morning found what they thought at first were turnips, but were in fact mangel-wurzels; chewy, tasteless vegetables used for cattle fodder. They tasted like straw and proved to be totally inedible. To make matters worse, the heavens opened and it rained non-stop for the next two days. They were soaked through, cold, hungry and thoroughly miserable. They had discussed the possibility of knocking on a cottage door, but the fear of being reported prevented them. The taller of the two Geordies spoke a little German and was generally optimistic about their chances, making light of what they were up against whenever it was possible. His mate, who Arthur had seen more of at the camp, was the opposite. He was all doom and gloom and was convinced every hour was their last before being recaptured. Arthur quickly tired of his moaning.

Their plan to keep out of sight during the day worked well; they never once saw nor heard anybody. After a few days of little if anything to eat, Arthur was as downhearted as he could remember being. One morning, they stood on the brow of a hill and looked down on the valley below. To the left was a small village. They decided that they had no choice but to go into the village and give themselves up. If it meant they would be returned to Auschwitz they would have to accept it. The alternative was to starve to death.

They had passed road signs indicating that they were now in Czechoslovakia, but had no idea of the name of the village. It was, however, very small and in the middle of nowhere. They thought it unlikely there would be a German presence. They made their way along a path that led through a gate and on to a road. They were close to the first of the buildings when they were confronted by a policeman carrying a gun. When challenged, the tall Geordie answered in German that they were Czech refugees. The officer then asked a barrage of questions in his native tongue to which Geordie, smiling by this time, was totally unable to respond.

The officer led them to the village hall where they admitted to being escaping British POWs from Auschwitz. The officer then immediately called the German authorities, but had the decency to see the men were well-fed and given the facilities to wash. They told the policeman about the treatment being handed out to the Jews at Auschwitz: the slave labour, the brutality, the absence of food and, of course, the gas chambers and the murders. The officer nodded his head grimly. They told him nothing, it seemed, he did not already know.

They had expected to be picked up within a few hours, but by the end of the day there was still no sign of the Germans. They bedded down for the night and waited again the next day. They were well fed and well treated, and although they were objects of curiosity for the local villagers, they were met with nothing but hospitality and additional gifts of food. They were treated with respect by the authorities and the officer escorted them around the village for exercise; they were given a pack of cards, a dartboard and a small billiard table for their entertainment and the food was better than anything they had tasted since they left home. Their accommodation was also more than satisfactory.

There was no news from the German authorities and the days passed. The fact that they would sooner or later be returned to Auschwitz played heavily on their nerves, but they made the most of the kindness they received from the folk of the Czech village.

As it happened, two full weeks passed before the Germans arrived.

CHAPTER TWELVE

It was an emotional departure from the village. They had no idea what awaited them back at the camp, but they feared the worst. The journey took the best part of two days and they were mostly quiet for the entire time. Adding to their fears was the thought that they might be considered collaborators in the attempted break-out from the Jewish camp and suffer accordingly. The prolonged periods of silence between the three men without doubt heightened the tension in the back of that German truck, so much so that Arthur was certain a stranger would have felt capable of cutting the atmosphere with the proverbial knife. Suddenly the vehicle came to a stop seemingly in the middle of nowhere and for no apparent reason. Petrified glances were exchanged between the Brits, each of whom had heard that stopping in a deserted spot was a popular German habit prior to extinguishing Allied lives. Imagine the POWs' reaction when the realisation hit them that the stoppage was merely to relieve German bladders.

Arriving back at Monowitz, they climbed from the lorry and shook each other's hands, fully expecting that this would be the last time they would see each other. They were, however, left at the gate and told to return to their huts and await further orders. This surprised them. Arthur was in a different hut from the two Geordies and walking back alone he did not know what was happening.

There was only one other man in the hut as he entered and he hardly raised an eyebrow at his appearance.

'How did it go then?' he asked casually. This was no way to greet a man who had been on the run and recaptured. Arthur's mind was racing.

'Oh, all right,' he answered cautiously. It suddenly dawned on Arthur that nobody was aware that they had, in fact, escaped. Why? There could be only one reason and Arthur went to leave the hut, knowing that he had to warn his Geordie friends before they let the cat out of the bag. He didn't get as far as the door when one of them came rushing in.

'Arthur,' he said, quietly but urgently, 'keep your mouth shut! Everybody thinks we've been on a working party!'

'I know,' Arthur replied, 'it can only mean one thing. It's a Wehrmacht cover-up. If the SS get wind of the fact we escaped, we won't be the only ones in for the high jump. Some senior German officers will be in trouble, too.'

'You're right! They're going to pretend nothing's happened!'

After all they had been through since being recaptured, they could barely contain themselves at their good fortune. It had never crossed Arthur's mind that he might step down from the lorry and walk straight back to the hut as if nothing had happened.

'Arthur, where have you been? What have you been doing?'

Arthur could hear the childlike but sincere greeting from a distressed Alan Blades as he entered the hut. The disturbed lad hugged his minder and Arthur was choked at the show of affection and the realisation of his responsibility towards his Norfolk friend. Apparently his nigh-on three-week absence had caused Alan immeasurable torment.

Sergeant-Major Charlie Coward had a very different style to his predecessor Innes. Innes would not allow them to work in the railway sidings at the Buna plant, it being deemed as a direct contravention of the Geneva Convention. Coward, however, was only too happy for the men to work there, seeing it as an excellent opportunity for sabotage: stones and sand found their way into axle boxes, holes appeared in carriage roofs, damaging important equipment, and destination plates were swapped so that vital supplies for the Eastern Front ended up in Holland, while hundreds of tins of paint were sent to the Russian front.

More and more, they saw American Flying Fortress aircraft passing overhead on bombing raids. Each time, the air-raid siren would sound and the managers of the factories and the guards would run for the shelters, often allowing the POWs to make up their own minds whether or not they followed them. On one occasion, the siren came as an I. G. Farben engineer arrived at the camp on his BMW motorbike, which he rolled on its side and left as he ran for cover. The temptation was too much for Arthur. He cranked up the bike and rode it around the internal roads of the camp. When he put it back, he let down the tyres and put dirt in the petrol tank. As he returned to his mates, he was clapped and cheered all the way.

The German engineer who owned the BMW called Arthur and five of his fellow POWs to one side one day and told them that the pipes they had installed were to be pressure tested. If the tests were failed, they would be shot. The engineer was aware that the half-dozen men in front of him had been solely responsible for the sabotage and the Germans were obviously tiring of their repeated attempts at disruption. The men knew the game was up. The piping had not the remotest chance of passing even the most insignificant of pressure tests. They had each filled them with an assortment of stones and dirt and Arthur himself had fitted two blank flanges.

The SS officer who Arthur had crossed on his first day at work had arrived on the scene and as far as Arthur was concerned, the game was up. Within minutes, he would be shot. Natasha came over to Little Darkie. She knew what they had been up to and realised that he too would soon be dead.

The engineers were preparing the test and as they did so, Arthur's heart beat like a piston as his life and loved ones once more came to mind. At St Valery and Bardiyah, his life had flashed before him as he thought he would die at any moment. Though the circumstances were very different, Arthur was this time sure that nothing could save them, and the images from home once again came vividly to mind.

Suddenly, the air-raid siren sounded and the pressure test had to be delayed. It was but a short respite for the men. When the aircraft were gone, they would return to the factory and the test would be restarted. Everybody was ordered into the shelters. The fact that their shelter was totally inadequate for the purpose for which it was being used hardly seemed to matter to the six condemned men it contained. They talked nervously to each other and waited for the dreaded all-clear.

Just at that moment they heard the unmistakable swishing sound of falling bombs, followed by a deafening explosion. Everybody was surprised by this turn of events. In every previous case, the aircraft had flown back from their raids empty. It could only be assumed that maybe the bomb had been stuck and the plane had only just been able to free its deadly load.

Whatever the cause, the plane passed and the all-clear siren sounded. This usually welcome sound brought no relief to the men awaiting the pressure test. Arthur had, at the most, fifteen minutes left to live.

The doors to the shelter were opened and Arthur in his turn shuffled outside. The sight that greeted him took his breath away. One of the bombs had gone straight through the roof of BAU 38, blowing away the entire gable end. Dozens of distorted pipes swung freely in the air and smoke hung over the factory in a dark cloud. Looking around what he could see of the twenty-five square miles of Auschwitz, only one building had been hit and it was the one in which the fateful pressure test was about to take place. The six doomed men had to contain their joy, but their celebrations were loud and long once they were back in their huts. Up to that time, no bombs had been dropped on the camp, but the first time it happened was to Arthur the greatest living proof of divine intervention.

From that day forth, the Germans introduced a clever ruse to limit the damage of any air-raids. Whenever the bombers were passing they released a dense fog from cylinders loaded on to the backs of trucks. These vehicles were parked in insignificant parts of the camp, but gave the impression they had something to hide. Bombs would then be directed at these areas. As successful as it was, it was very much a case of closing the stable door after the horse had bolted as the BAU 38 building, one of the most important sites on the camp, was now destroyed forever.

CHAPTER THIRTEEN

There were a couple of illicit radios operating in the camp and by May 1944, it had become clear from the broadcasts that Germany was losing the war. This sparked an increase in the extermination of the Jewish prisoners, most of whom were Hungarian. As many as 65,000 would arrive at the camp in one day, with something in the region of 5,000 crammed on to one train of 50 carriages. Eight trains arrived each day, followed by another five every night.

In order to appease the new arrivals, they were led to believe they were being resettled in the area and some were even told they were being exchanged for German POWs via the Red Cross. Thus assured, they were led quietly to the gas chambers, only realising the deceit when it was too late. Arthur heard that such was the volume of the genocide that even an SS guard could bear it no longer. Working in close proximity to the gas chambers, he went out of his mind and was unceremoniously gassed himself.

A new arrival was placed in Arthur's hut; he went by the name of Evans and immediately began to arouse suspicion. He was both well-spoken and well-educated, but also remarkably well-fed. His intelligence quickly earned him the nickname 'Professor'. He said that he had been an assistant pathologist in

Canada to one of the country's leading surgeons but, like most tales in Auschwitz, the story was treated with scepticism.

Sometime in the late summer of 1944 uniformed Wehrmacht officers from outside the camp brought to every Allied hut leaflets entitled, 'Join Up and Fight Against the Russians'. The British were being asked to join the Eastern Freedom Fighters, to wage another war alongside the perpetrators of these inhuman atrocities. The unanimous chorus of boos and cat-calls gave the desperate enquirers the answer they did not want to hear. Certain factions of other nationalities did succumb to the Nazi propaganda and in that same year the German Regular Army and the SS had light infantry divisions of so-called Eastern volunteers. A few other divisions and brigades of Norwegian, French, Dutch and Albanian nationalists also fought on the side of the swastika. Arthur and his colleagues were also similarly pestered at their place of work but, to his knowledge, no British POW defected to the Nazi cause.

News of the war improved further as autumn approached and it was decided to hold a Gala Day. Arthur joined up with Taffy's choir, the members of which approached their rehearsals with a dedication and enthusiasm normally reserved for the Llangollen Eisteddfod. Reports of more Allied victories added to the buoyancy of the preparations and at times it was difficult to believe that they were amid such death and perversion. On the day of the gala, a coconut shy, a small roundabout, and a number of ingeniously constructed side-shows had been erected. In the evening, a pantomime was to be held. The gala would have been a great success, but for the occurrence of the greatest tragedy to strike the British POWs during their internment.

The date was 20 August 1944. Early in the afternoon, as the men were enjoying themselves, they were interrupted by the air-raid sirens and as the camp was now being bombed on a regular basis, the men made their way to the brick-built shelters, entered via a sloping ramp and closed off by steel doors. Arthur was with Spud Murphy from Northwich, ready to close the doors once the men from the huts allocated to that shelter were inside. Just as the doors were shut, they heard an almighty swishing sound followed by a tremendous explosion. The ground shook and the far end of the shelter caved in as it took a direct hit.

Inside the shelter were some 150 POWs and nearly all were at least injured in some way. Arthur and Spud immediately opened the doors. Inside was thick with dust and Arthur heard a shout from the far end calling for any miners among the men. Both Spud and Arthur thought that they had urinated in their clothing, but closer examination showed it to be the blood from a multitude of tiny shrapnel wounds.

Within a few moments, a number of blond, blue-eyed members of the Hitler Youth arrived on the scene and worked as hard as anyone in the hours that followed to free those prisoners buried beneath the rubble. A medical officer called Harrison operated on a young lad with a hole in his head the size of a tennis ball. He left him holding a clamp to the wound.

'Leave that in, son,' he told him, 'it'll help.'

Arthur helped another man carry the unfortunate lad outside and placed him onto a truck in which he and others badly injured were taken into hospital in Oswiecim. The rest of the day's events were cancelled and those still in the camp were left to mourn the loss of 15 comrades.

One of those lost was Big Darkie, the Royal Engineer from the Midlands, who had so impressed everybody with his ability to move the boilers around. He was a great thinker, a brilliant engineer and much admired. Another sad loss was Little Darkie from Essex, the lad in love with the Ukrainian girl, Natasha. For her, his death was sheer heartbreak. He had been her one shining light, giving her hope for the future and a reason to carry on. She was totally crushed when the news was given to her.

Arthur passed one of the huts and thought he heard a moaning sound. This was the hut where the pantomime would have been staged and on entering he saw that some of the internal apex timbers had come down with the force of the explosion. Underneath was Billy Griffith from Birmingham. He had ignored the sirens to finish working on the pantomime preparations and had paid for it. Finding him trapped beneath the fallen timbers, Arthur leaned across to see if he was OK and was met with the broadest of cheeky grins. Even in adversity, this natural comic could raise a smile and make the best of things.

'Bloomin' heck, Brummie,' Arthur said, 'you don't look like you've got much to smile about.'

'Oh, I don't know, Arthur,' he replied, 'it's the first time I ever brought the house down!'

It was a day they had waited for with great anticipation and it had ended in tragedy. It was heartbreaking to think that those 15 men had endured all they had only to be killed by the bombs from their own side. Severe injuries eventually pushed the number of deaths up to 38. This figure appeared in a German intelligence report, which was to be distributed in other POW camps in the Silesia district for propaganda purposes. In other words as proof of inhuman methods of warfare adopted by the American forces.

Once he was alone, Arthur wept unashamedly.

It was at this time that Evans, the pathologist's assistant, had the opportunity to prove that he was what he said he was and he did just that. Assisted by Harrison, he worked tirelessly among the more badly injured men. The death toll would have been much higher but for the skill and determination of the pair of them and afterwards the men signed a scroll of appreciation which was presented to them both.

The dead men were laid out for each survivor to pay his respects. Two days later a small service was held and the bodies were loaded on to a truck draped in the Union Jack flag. They were taken to the local parish cemetery in Oswiecim and buried beside a wall in a communal grave. Fifteen POWs were permitted to attend the burial. On 13 September 1944, the common grave was hit by a bomb dropped by the US Air Force during its bombing of the I. G. Farben works. It was completely destroyed.

At about half-past ten every other Tuesday, the men would hear a train pulling out loaded with fuel for the Eastern Front.

When Arthur had arrived at the camp in the spring of 1943, the Benzene plant in the far corner of the Buna complex was already in full operation. This plant must have played a major part in the advance on Russia. One day, an RAF plane flew over and dropped leaflets warning the Germans to cease the train's movements. The following Tuesday, the British POWs waited with excitement to see if the warning would be heeded, but the train left as usual.

The following night the bombers came and bombed the plant for a full hour. When the lads finally came out from the shelters, the fires caused by the void lit the night as if it were midday. Shortly afterwards, an RAF reconnaissance plane flew over and dipped its wings in salute of a successful mission. As the British contingent jumped up and down and cheered, they could clearly see the pilot raise his fist in determined acknowledgement. The men looked up to skies and Arthur was nudged by one of his fellow prisoners.

'Do you know what he's saying to us?'

Arthur looked at him and shook his head.

'He's saying, "Hang on down there, boys, we won't be long coming for you now."'

The sight of a fellow countryman was an enormous lift to everyone, but like many men in the camp, Arthur still could not believe that they would be allowed to live to tell the tale of what they had seen. As it happened, nobody came to liberate them. They would have to make their own way home.

CHAPTER FOURTEEN

Arthur was walking by the wire one evening after work when he saw a man limping past on the road that ran alongside the camp. As he got closer, he saw the man was a young German soldier returning from the Russian front. He looked no more than seventeen and had had his left foot blown off just above the ankle. The stub of his leg was swathed in filthy bandages and he hobbled along on improvised crutches made from tree branches. He was an ordinary young soldier, caught up in the madness of the times and Arthur could only feel great pity for him. It dismayed Arthur when the German guards did not even acknowledge him as he passed. He was never more certain that the Germans were staring down the barrel of defeat.

Slowly, more soldiers passed and they continued to do so over the next few days. Many had missing limbs, some were blind and being led by comrades. They dragged themselves along, their only objective to stay alive and make their way home to Germany.

The crematoria were busier than ever as the Christmas of 1944 approached and the stench of death was overpowering. Charlie Coward had been called back to Lamsdorf by its British camp leader, Sergeant-Major Sheriff, after the

Germans finally caught on to his surreptitious methods. He was transferred to Teschen for his own safety and was not replaced. Coward's manner of dressing-up and socialising with the German officers had not been appreciated by everyone and he earned himself the nickname the 'Count of Auschwitz'. He did, however, have his own way of getting the job done and was quite prepared to push his luck to the limit.

After being taken prisoner at Calais in 1940, Coward had managed to escape his captors twice before he had even arrived at his first POW camp. During his seven subsequent escapes he managed to be awarded the Iron Cross whilst hiding in a German Army field hospital, observed experimental V1 rockets and conceived to send coded information back to London. This informative matter consisted of anything of military value, the conditions of work for the civilians and inmates as well as British POWs, and also details of approximate numbers of Jews delivered to the gas chambers together with their country of origin. He was able to get out approximately six letters a week in his privileged position, always in the guise of writing to Mr William Orange, his already dead father. His wife, Florence, was at first confused by these letters and it took her a few months to realize William Orange stood for War Office and so redirected his mail accordingly.

After hostilities had ceased Coward made it clear at the Nuremburg trials that the civilian contractors could not be excused their dreadful part in this savage Auschwitz death factory enterprise. He never heard of any German foreman protesting against gassing providing it was for Jews. They looked upon the killing of this race as killing vermin. One particular foreman boasted to Coward on one occasion about having seen Jews arrive for gassing, one hundred to a railway wagon, standing because there was not enough room to sit down. It was too much trouble to take the inmates out, so a gas pipe was put into the wagon.

Although opinions of Coward's strengths varied somewhat markedly from within the ranks of his British charges, the Jewish race certainly paid great reverence to him. He is the only Englishman to have a tree planted in his honour in the Avenue of Righteous Gentiles in Vad Yashim and, apart from Winston Churchill, is the only other British recipient of the Israeli Peace medal.

The downturn in German fortunes was accompanied by an upsurge in SS brutality. Many Jews, obviously close to death, were forced to carry on by severe beatings. The behaviour of the kapos was all the more sickening, proving to what depths mankind can sink. They were only rewarded with their own single bunk and extra rations, but were prepared to torment and torture their fellow Jews, countrymen and women to get them.

There were exceptions. One kapo was a former American lawyer who had been trapped in Europe when visiting relatives at the beginning of the war. Arthur had befriended him over the previous few months after he had noticed subtle differences in his behaviour. When he was being observed by officers and guards of the SS, this kapo would rant and wave his stick with the worst of them, but Arthur noted that he would hit the ground or pull his blows as they landed. When he was not being watched he would cease his shouting and turn a blind eye to any bits of rations the soldiers passed to the Jews. He trod a fine and dangerous line, for his punishment would have been worse than death had he ever been caught. A short, thickset man, he was probably the only American POW in the camp, but his acting deserved a better stage and was to earn him life's ultimate Oscar: survival and freedom.

One of the last British POWs to arrive was a 'Farmer Giles' character from Somerset. He returned to the hut one evening upset at the news that he had been taking part in the manufacture of submarine torpedoes, clearly in conflict with the Geneva Convention. The lads in the hut thought he was off his trolley, but he insisted he had seen the torpedoes racked up in a storage hut by the I. G. Farben complex. The following day, he was escorted by senior managers of Farben and the SS to examine the contents of the hut in question. The men waited with apprehension, clearly expecting trouble. The 'torpedoes' turned out to be gas bottles and the men were never sure if the 'farmer' was as daft as he seemed or clever enough to dream up a ruse to disrupt the best part of a working day. In a consensus of opinion, few chose the latter.

Snow began to fall and more and more wounded German soldiers trudged past the camp. The soldiers of the Wehrmacht became increasingly disheartened and there was less supervision taking place in the factory. Arthur's weight had dropped from ten stone at the beginning of the war to six and food was as scarce as it had ever been. The situation was made the more critical by the complete absence by this time of Red Cross food parcels. They were restricted to just one diminishing piece of black bread and a ladle of soup given to them at noon each day. After that, they had nothing but an occasional cup of the coffee substitute.

Arthur was on the third reading of his Bible from cover to cover and he was frequently abused for sticking so determinedly to his faith. Those who knew him better would leave him be when he was quietly reading, but others would taunt him.

'Where's your God now?' they would call to him, but Arthur ignored them. He knew that without his faith, he could not have endured the last couple of years. God, he believed, had been beside him every moment of his life. He noted that the same men who questioned the existence of his God were the same men who clenched their hands and thanked God for their deliverance after the shelter had been bombed.

Being some distance from the Jewish section, the British soldiers could only hear the small orchestra that would play as the victims filed into the gas chambers if the wind blew towards them. One evening, they could hear some commotion outside and went out to see that the latest arrivals had been forced to leave the train early due to bomb damage of the line. There were some one thousand old men, women and children walking on the other side of the wire. The children were playing and singing and their mothers tried to smile for their sake. Once they were gone, the men returned to their hut in complete silence. They knew what the fate of those people would be. A Pole confirmed the following morning that every single one of those people, including the children, had been gassed during the night.

In the New Year, news was rife in the camp that the Russians were not very far away. The men looked up the road on the far side of the wire almost as if they expected the Russians to appear at any moment. The SS guards were running around like demented lunatics and the POWs made a concerted effort to keep clear of them. In addition, strong rumours of cannibalism amongst the Mongolian race in the Russian camp did nothing to soothe the tattered nerves prevalent in that supercharged atmosphere existing in the weeks approaching liberation. Next came the first raid from Russian aircraft, dropping their devastating anti-personnel bombs for more than an hour. The shrapnel would scythe across the ground up to head height and instantly kill anyone in its path. They went on for three days, keeping the starving prisoners in the frozen shelter for hour after hour.

News came through that Krakow had been taken, which meant they were very close. This was followed with wild rumours that the SS were to destroy the camp and everyone in it. The first thing that happened though, was a relief to everyone when on 15 January, a number of Jewish prisoners were moved west. This was the first positive indication that the SS did not intend a mass general slaughter of survivors before their departure.

As they left, they did not look able to walk more than a mile or two and given that they would be out all night in temperatures of eighteen degrees below freezing without shelter, Arthur did not believe many, if any, would be alive the following morning. Those left behind were not convinced they would not be shot or blown up.

One morning, Maria, the Polish girl with whom he'd become close, came looking for Arthur. She was with a Ukrainian girl and beckoned for him to follow them to the eastern end of the complex. It was obvious that the men were not to be put to work on this morning, so Arthur followed. He was led to the upper floor of a building he had not been to before. Maria raised a finger to her lips and quietly the three peered through a window, keeping themselves as much out of sight as possible.

In the yard below, SS guards were shouting and whipping a number of Jews who were being forced to throw the carcasses of dozens of their dead comrades into a large bonfire. The ground on which the fire was built had been hollowed out and so the bodies and materials were being thrown down on to the flames. Suddenly, Arthur was horrified to see small children being brought into the yard. He felt the bile rise in his throat as the children were kicked and booted on to the fire. Their screams were more than Arthur could bear. He turned away, his heart pounding in his chest. He believed that during the past two years he had been witness to every depravity of which man was capable, but now he shook violently at the scene before him. Auschwitz was in its death throes, but in its final hours was able to produce a sickening horror beyond his comprehension and imagination. Arthur staggered back towards his hut, his mind racing, the screams of the children still ringing in his ears. For several hours Arthur could not speak and it would be many years before he could describe to others what he had seen.

Sadly, he never saw Maria Kostka again. In the madness of the time, it was difficult to keep a track of where anybody was and whether or not Maria survived is not known to Arthur to this day. Over the years, he has thought of her many times. He had a genuine fondness for her and wonders if she was able to free herself from the insanity that enveloped the camp in the final days. He will never know.

Two crematoria were blown up as the sound of the Russian artillery could be heard in the distance. The fires raged all over the camp as much of the evidence of the atrocities, including the paperwork, was destroyed. It was also a very dangerous time as SS guards went on a demented binge of murder. The British POWs stayed out of the way and kept an eye on the movements of any SS guards. Most of the civilian staff and workers had disappeared and the anxiety affected the more decent Wehrmacht guards who feared the arrival of the approaching Russian infantry.

The tension that night was almost unbearable. The men knew they were close to surviving the horrors they had been subjected to for the best part of two years, but they did not know what was to happen next. Their lives could be taken from them at any moment. In the middle of the night, the air-raid sirens sounded and the men rushed from the huts to the shelters. Many left precious personal belongings behind, but they were never to see the inside of the huts again. They were pinned down in the shelters for three days by the Russian Air Force, the attacks coming thick and fast. Some lasted a full hour and some were only ten minutes apart. It was during these raids that the grieving Natasha, Little

Darkie's sweetheart, was killed. Those who ventured a look into the compound during a lull confirmed that the huts had all been destroyed. This was undoubtedly a preliminary attack that would come before the main assault.

CHAPTER FIFTEEN

After the third day of bombardment, there was a prolonged period of quiet and finally German guards appeared and told them to collect what belongings they had and parade by the main gate. It was 23 January 1945.

The men had what they stood up in, most of their property having been destroyed. For Arthur, this meant he had no balaclava or gloves. On reaching the gates, they found them wide open with about ten guards standing about. The last Jewish roll-call had taken place some six days earlier and they had been removed from the camp. It was still five-thirty in the morning but in the darkness they could see the damage caused by the bombers.

Snow was thick on the ground and the sound of the Russian artillery and infantry seemed so close Arthur expected the lead tanks to appear at any moment. He looked around at the bedraggled appearance of his emaciated comrades and doubted the ability of many to survive in the sub-zero temperatures. Arthur was dressed in full uniform and a greatcoat, but the size eight shoes he normally wore had fallen from his feet and he had managed to procure a pair of size elevens in the shelter. He had no socks and instead his feet were wrapped in strips of an old shirt, helping his feet to fit his newly acquired footwear. The fact that his feet were given so much space was a comfort.

There were some 230 Allied POWs and finally, as they wondered what was happening, they were approached by the senior Wehrmacht officer, Feldwebel Messer. They listened to his words with a great deal of apprehension.

He told the men assembled that they were free to leave the camp; they were no longer prisoners of war. They could, he advised, march to the west towards the British and American forces, in which case, they would be accompanied by the soldiers of the Wehrmacht who would surrender. Or they could walk the short distance to the east where before long they would be met by the advancing Russians.

For Arthur, his mind was made up in no time at all. He did not fancy his chances with the Russians. They had no idea what kind of reception they would be given and had heard tales of the Russians dealing with all POWs as potential spies. He decided he would face the long walk towards the advancing British and American lines. If nothing else he would be, God willing, nearer home with every step he took.

All but four Scottish lads took the road west and a story came back later that they were mown down by Russian tanks as they stepped in front of them waving their arms. The Russians were under direct orders from the Kremlin to get to Berlin first and anybody in their way was brushed aside. The story was never confirmed, but he never heard from any of the four again. Arthur was to later discover the Russians did not arrive in Auschwitz for another four days.

As the men set out, they did not know how far they would have to walk, but nobody was under any illusions that it would be less than several hundred miles. Arthur set off in a group with Corporals Jim Purdy and Cummins, taking it in turns to look after Alan Blades, who was in a sorry state. They took an abandoned cart from the camp and pushed it through the snow.

They covered some ten miles on the first day despite having nothing to eat, and spent the night in a barn. There was, apparently, a German Hauptman travelling in front trying to arrange what accommodation he could for the men behind. Temperatures dropped to 22 degrees below zero in what was Poland's coldest winter for many years. They set off the following morning at about four o'clock and had to walk over hundreds of dead Jews strewn across the road, partially covered in snow. Some had died of the cold, but others had clearly been shot in the head.

The column of men rested for ten minutes in each hour, but Arthur would have preferred to carry on, finding it very difficult to restart each time. In the course of the next twenty hours, they would cover nearly forty miles. Most of the men were beginning to suffer from frostbite of the fingers, toes and ears and some gave up the march, collapsing to the side of the road to die. There was a man known to Arthur simply as Sergeant Andy, who walked up and down the line encouraging the men to carry on. He would tell them that there was food and warm shelter waiting for them at their daily destination. Sometimes his resolve wore thin on the men struggling in the line, but as the Germans were determined to put as many miles between themselves and the Russians, his constant cajoling kept many men alive.

Arthur was free of frostbite, but every time he closed his eyes his eyelids froze and he had to rub them vigorously to get them open. At the end of the second day, they turned off the main road and walked up a tree-lined avenue. To one side was a large guest house and they were received by a man who plied them with hot soup, bread and ersatz coffee. Such was the relief at the warmth of the food that Arthur was close to tears.

Arthur was somewhat surprised that he had not suffered from frostbite, for when it was his turn to push the cart he had no protective gloves. He had, though, befriended a man who was suffering badly with both feet. Arthur stayed up with him all night as he wept with pain, but by the following morning it was obvious that he could not continue. Their host promised he would be taken to hospital.

After the exertions of the previous day, they did not resume the march until noon and no longer came across the bodies of dead Jews, most of the SS by this time having taken a different route. They marched for just a few hours and yet still an increasing number were forced to drop out or fall behind. Arthur took a position at the back of the column but they were repeatedly stopped by their efforts to persuade comrades to continue. Those they left behind were unlikely to survive.

They stopped at a barn, but there was no food awaiting them. They hunted around and found what at first they thought were potatoes but turned out to be mangel-wurzels.

The following day began at five in the morning and though they knew they were in for a long day, it was clear and they were warmed by the sun still low in the sky. Some of the men attempted to sing, no doubt inspired by Sergeant Andy, but it did not last long. In his walking up and down the line, Andy was still walking three times further than anybody else. He had made so many unfulfilled promises of food, little attention was now paid to him or his references to the White Ladies (the Red Cross lorries), but he carried on nonetheless.

The days passed and they reached Troppua and continued following the German guards, assuming they knew where they were going. Just outside the village they were attacked by a single Russian fighter plane and scattered in all directions. It transpired that the only ones injured were those who left the road and Arthur and his immediate company decided in future to drop to the floor where they were if they were attacked in such a fashion again.

They had been marching for three weeks when they were next attacked, this time by a number of Russian fighters. The column again scattered and many, despite the waving of white cloths, were killed or badly wounded. This was a tragic end for those who had suffered so much and were so near to freedom. Although he had dropped to the floor straight away, the spray of bullets had missed Arthur by a few feet and caught instead a young Geordie with whom Arthur had been walking.

The dead had their identity discs removed and were left by the roadside for someone else to bury. The effect on the column of being strafed by the aircraft of those purporting to be on the same side was severe. They were sitting ducks in the face of such attacks and the loss of close friends hung heavy over the men as they trudged on their way.

The Russian planes never came back. It was assumed they had opened fire on seeing the column led by German guards, but had pulled away on realising that they were followed by Allied soldiers. Periodically, the column was stopped while those unable to continue were made comfortable at the side of the road and left. Their fate was out of their hands, but few if any would have lived for long.

One evening they came across a concrete building that had housed Russian POWs and was fitted with bunk beds and mattresses. Many of the weary men fell gratefully on to them, but Arthur held back. He sensed the bunks were alive with bugs and dreaded the discomfort they could cause on the rest of the march. Life in captivity had generated in Arthur an ability to detect the presence of those tiny tormentors. He tried to warn the others but generally his words went unheeded.

That night he shared a groundsheet outside the building with one of the German guards and in the morning his caution proved to be justified, many of the men suffering from swollen eyelids where they had been bitten. They ate something they called potato soup, but which contained nothing they could recognise. Afterwards, what remained of the column continued, minus two guards who had left during the night, no doubt believing they would make greater progress unhindered.

By this time, Andy's promises of food were usually met with a chorus of obscenities but around noon on that day, they came across a party of Czechoslovakian nuns, dressed in white, standing alongside a van. They were served with plates of beans, tea and coffee, and because the nuns had probably expected there to be more in the party than by now there was, Arthur and the other men were for the first time in two years able to eat as much as they could. The van was picked clean of all it contained and as if this was not joy enough, the nuns reassured them they would be waiting for them again further on their journey. Sergeant Andy was elevated to near saintly status and he was never verbally abused again.

Some of the men had eaten too much and their emaciated frames and shrunken bellies could not cope with this sudden feast. Many stopped to be sick at the side of the road. Guards and British soldiers continued to disappear, but no attempt was made to stop anybody. Participation on the march was entirely voluntary and those who fancied their chances alone were able to leave. Arthur decided that with so many desperate German units roaming the area, safety behind the guards was all-important. We need them now, he thought, as much as they will need us when we reach our destination.

CHAPTER SIXTEEN

By the end of March 1945, they emerged from the forests and rural plains on to a major road leading to Prague. The weather was kinder and the availability of vegetables improved. Each night they would break into the hog enclosures and steal what potatoes and turnips they required. The handcart, which they had been tempted to ditch so many times, became a godsend.

The produce was boiled up and shared with the guards, men of the Wehrmacht, with whom they had shared as fellow men their plight over the previous eight weeks. For tobacco the men would dry the leaves of flowers in their pockets and roll them between any pieces of paper they could find for a cigarette. Arthur, who preferred his pipe, would experiment with different varieties of leaves, crushing them into the pipe bowl and making a mental note of which gave the most satisfying smoke. What little comfort such inhalation provided was always accompanied by streaming eyes.

On one occasion, they had no fuel to light a fire and with great reluctance Arthur donated his treasured Bible to the meagre pile of fuel they had mustered. Watching the flames licking through the wafer-thin pages was akin to the cremation of a dear friend, but Arthur felt that God had blessed his action.

His journey through Hell was near its end and the Bible had served its purpose, delivering him sound of mind and body.

They arrived in Prague and crossed Wenceslas Square, where they were met by people cheering and offering them food and drink. They were grateful for the food, knowing that the Czech capital had had a hard time of it during the Nazi occupation and the people had little to give away. Corporal Cummings was pushing the handcart when he was beckoned by an old lady holding a huge loaf of bread. The loaf was the size of a bin lid and Cummings sent Arthur to collect what must have been near worth its weight in gold in those hard times. The woman was dressed in a long black skirt and wore a small hat. Arthur thanked her from the bottom of his heart and the lady simply smiled and pushed him back towards his friends.

Moments later a shout went up.

'Look out, Arthur!'

Before he could turn, he was hit violently from behind and knocked out. When he came round some considerable time later he was reassured to see the loaf was by his side on the cart. He was later told he had been hit by one of the German guards who had a short while earlier heard his family had been wiped out in an air-raid of British bombers. The man had been Messer's personal clerk at the camp and Arthur consoled himself with the fact that he was probably the man who typed up the report that he had been on a working party when in fact he had escaped. Later that day, the man disappeared, no doubt to make his way more directly back home.

They left Prague walking alongside a railtrack running parallel to the road. Up ahead was a train, its wagons filled with military equipment. Suddenly, RAF planes screamed down on the train and it was blown to the sky. As they passed the wreckage, they saw the remains of the unmanned rockets that terrorised London in the last stages of the war. They talked about the raid for the best part of the day, the sight of the RAF helping them to believe that they just might make it home after all.

They came to Marianske Lazne and as they entered the square they were confronted by a mountain of currency. The marks were piled high, unattended in the centre of the square. There were few people about and the one person who seemed to be in charge was a rounded, bubbly woman in her late forties and dressed in a smart burgundy costume. She told them they had robbed the bank of these worthless marks and invited the men to help themselves before she set light to them.

For Arthur, this was nothing short of plunder and he would take no part in it, but those who did were to benefit after the war. Far from the marks being worthless, they were bought off the soldiers for considerable sums of money when they got back home.

They crossed the border into Germany and came across the beautiful town of Weiden, a place totally unspoiled by the ravages of a war that had destroyed so many parts of Europe. The local inhabitants came out of their little houses and gaped with curiosity at the motley crew that passed before them. They were friendly and, more importantly generous, supplying the men with meat and bread. It was a surreal world they had entered, as if the war was just a distorted figment of their demented imaginations. The people emerged from the immaculate, serene houses, dressed in a style unfamiliar to the gaze and seeming to belong to another age.

They were escorted to what seemed to be the town hall and were served real coffee. Shortly afterwards, the town's Burgermeister took them to a room where there was an assortment of weaponry and military equipment, including some binoculars of the finest quality laid out on long trestle tables. They were told arrangements had been made with the Americans to hand in all known weapons to one central collection point prior to the town being taken. In this way, further unnecessary bloodshed was avoided.

They stayed in the town for a couple of days. They were shown the large houses on the outskirts, some of which had been occupied by SS soldiers on leave where they were encouraged by those higher up the Nazi hierarchy to sleep with local blue-eyed, blonde women of the area to help produce Germany's future. Despite evidence of Hitler's empire crumbling all around him, there were many beautiful German women in the town in the last stages of pregnancy, ready to produce the next generation of the Reich. They left the town and within two hours, unbelievably, they heard American bombers pass overhead and a minute later the sound of the beautiful town being bombed.

Over the next three days they marched a further 42 miles and reached Regensberg, where they were divided and billeted in different smallholdings. Corporal Cummings and Arthur stayed together as they had for the whole journey and were put to work with others filling in craters around the rail station. Alan Blades was excused all duties and was left in a barn with the one remaining German soldier still with them.

Their diet over the next few days consisted mostly of potatoes, although one morning Cummings caught a chicken as it walked over his bed. Within minutes, it was plucked and boiled up for breakfast. Strictly speaking, the town was still occupied by the Germans, but the Americans were on the other side of the Danube and ready to take it. On the second full day they were there, an American officer arrived in a jeep driven by a GI. He told them that the US Army would be in the town within a day or two, but in the meantime not to be lulled into a false sense of security by the apparent serenity that surrounded them.

'Keep your heads down and don't light any fires,' he told them. 'This ain't no time to slip up. You guys have been through enough already, I guess.'

They continued working on the craters, meeting more and more prisoners making their way back from other POW camps. That night, they saw a light aircraft passing overhead and then noticed a wisp of smoke coming from a building a short distance away. The plane was giving an exact location of the fire to the US artillery on the other side of the river and a few seconds the target was hit by shellfire. For the sake of brewing up, some two dozen former POWs were killed that evening within twenty-four hours of being liberated.

There was another raid the following day, but this time evasive action was taken and nobody else was killed. They sat together that night, in the company of the one remaining German guard, and talked about the following day, a day most of them thought they would never see. They lay awake all night, too excited to sleep. The Americans would soon be with them. They would soon be free.

CHAPTER SEVENTEEN

It was six o'clock on, appropriately enough for Arthur, a Sunday morning when they heard it. So quietly at first and then unmistakably came the squeaking, rumbling noise of approaching tanks. One by one, the men were roused and soon the whispers turned to shouts and the shouts to cheers.

'It's the Yanks, lads! It's the Yanks!'

They rushed outside and into the road to greet their liberators. The Americans dropped from their tanks and trucks and the men embraced. 'K' rations were thrown amongst them, each labelled breakfast, lunch or dinner. There were pots of jam, bars of chocolate, butter, biscuits and packets of cigarettes. It was too much for the men to take in. Arthur and many of those alongside him wept without shame.

Arthur ate the food and let the feeling of freedom and safety wash over him. The exhilaration of knowing he could for the first time for so long look forward to the rest of his life was almost too much. He had been close to death too many times to count and he fell to his knees in thanksgiving.

They were approached by the officer they had seen a couple of days earlier and told they would be taken to Straubing, an airport to the south of Regensberg, from where they would be airlifted to the west. Arthur volunteered to drive the tractor that transported the men on a trailer to the airport. The tractor was an old, dilapidated beast that Arthur had to fight every yard of the way, but he was happy to do what he could to get everybody safely to the airport. Some of the lads were in a sorry state and he doubted if they had long to live.

As the men waited, Arthur spoke to the American officer and asked that Alan Blades be given priority and the officer readily agreed. Dakotas landed with supplies and took the men out in turn, some flying first to Brussels and the more fortunate ones going straight back to England.

After four days, Arthur's turn came. He sat in the Dakota, twelve men to each side, and they listened as each of the square plastic windows popped as the plane became pressurised. The relief Arthur felt at finally being on his way home disappeared as he looked out of the window and saw flames coming from the starboard wing. He anxiously asked one of the flight officers if he knew one of the engines was on fire, but the man was unconcerned.

'The skipper will soon have that out,' he said.

Suddenly the plane lost altitude as if it was dropping out of the sky and each of the former POWs froze in terror. Within seconds the plane levelled and the fire in the wing was out. More than one in the company made use of the paper bags that had been provided on boarding.

Arthur arrived in Brussels on 8 May 1945, VE Day. Making his way through the city, thousands of people were celebrating in the street. By pure chance, he bumped into Fred Robinson, an old school friend, and they made the most of the joyous occasion. After six years of fear, never knowing what tomorrow would bring or indeed if there would be a tomorrow, it was wonderful to be among so many people of so many nationalities celebrating the first day of the future.

Arthur and Fred's celebrations were cut short when they were arrested by two military policemen for being improperly dressed. The fact that they had been POWs for more than two years cut no ice and they spent the night in a cell. The matter was put right the following morning on production of their pay books and after receiving profuse apologies from the officer in charge they were driven out to the airport. They were met by the sight of a line of magnificent Lancaster bombers and it gladdened their hearts to be going home in such style.

They had taken off and were over the channel before Arthur was aware they were airborne. He got to a window and watched as they flew over the white cliffs of Dover, a sight that brought tears to his eyes. They landed at Guildford, in Surrey, and were met by the WVS with cups of hot tea and broad smiles. Arthur's heart was near to bursting and though he must have looked as if he was at death's door, inside he felt like a million dollars. Alongside the WVS were those other stalwarts of the cause, the Salvation Army, offering all the returning POWs a pre-printed postcard informing worrying families of their return to Great Britain. The lads filled in the address details together with a personal message and the Post Office did the necessary.

He left for home the following day, travelling by way of London and Crewe. All he could think of was home and how he would decorate his father's house. He had received no word from home for the best part of three years so he had no idea what to expect, but he was excited at the thought of once again seeing familiar places and faces.

They say that the last mile home is the longest and so it proved for Arthur. His legs could barely carry him the remaining yards to his home. It was a joyful sight as it came into view, but approaching it, Arthur had a sixth sense that all was not right. This was reinforced when he noticed that people watched him from curtains when he would have expected them to come to the door to greet him and welcome him home.

As he walked up the path, he could see the house had not changed one bit since he had left it early in the war, but he felt apprehensive as he knocked and waited for an answer. The woman who came to the door was a complete stranger to him. He looked at her, but said nothing.

'You're Arthur, aren't yer?' she barked.

'Yes,' he replied.

'Well, you're not wanted here!' she snapped back before slamming the door in his face. He had not expected flags and bunting, but neither was he prepared for this. His father, he knew, was in the house, but had not had the nerve to come and face him. After standing for a minute rooted to the spot, he turned away and walked back up the path without looking around, making his way to his sister-in-law Margaret's small cottage in the next street.

She gave him a welcome fit for a king and fussed around him until he was near smothered in her kindness. She told him his father had married a woman from Liverpool a year earlier and they had already had a child. It had seemed that his father had allowed himself to be dominated by the woman and had not stood up to her when she laid down her laws. Arthur, despite his faith, was bitter towards him.

He had four months leave to sort himself out, but he found it difficult to talk with anyone. He spent hours each day walking and thinking about what he had been through. He would sit on the banks of the Weaver deep in thought, tossing stones into the river. The close friends he had made who had died in the camp and others who had not made it on that 700-mile march to freedom were very much in his thoughts.

Deep depression had set in and he thought of taking his life. He had considered throwing himself into the river but his excellent swimming prowess would instinctively save him. One day whilst walking past Hartford's blue bridge towards Northwich he noticed a small pile of pebbles, probably left over from recent maintenance work. He sat on the grass bank tossing them into the waterway and watched, mesmerised, by the ripples they produced. Then a strange phenomenon occurred that he cannot explain even to this day. Two swans he had passed some distance back swam towards him, thinking food was available. They soon realised they were unlucky as the pebbles sank. Both elegant creatures were pristine white; their grace and beauty making Arthur question his thoughts of suicide. One of them came out of the water and laid his head on Arthur's shoulder for a full minute or so. Arthur's initial response was of apprehension for his visitor's hissing anger was legendary. It was as though the swan appreciated Arthur's frame of mind and the former Auschwitz resident was moved to tears. The swan eventually dropped back into the water, waggling its rear feathers as it glided back to the bridge.

Arthur felt he had let them down and promptly went to Davenham, a local village, to buy some bread that he fed to the graceful and grateful pair. This extraordinary incident helped Arthur Dodd come to terms with the challenges of living the rest of his life. The first time Arthur retold this incident his eyes misted over as he choked on the words, 'It was a beautiful moment… a beautiful moment.'

His optimum weight before the war had been ten and a half stone, but he tipped the scales at just six stone ten when he got back. Within a few weeks he noticed a multitude of small sores breaking out on his legs. He recalled the MO at Auschwitz had warned him after the air-raid shelter was bombed that he might have many shrapnel wounds in his legs that would surface in their own time.

As he was still the responsibility of the Army, his own doctor would not treat him, so he reported to the MO of the nearest unit which was at the field bakery at Blakemere, Sandiway. The doctor paid little attention to Arthur's problem and listed him as 'M & D', meaning 'medicine and duties' and generally regarded as a shorthand for 'swinging the lead' or pretending to be ill.

As Arthur left the surgery, he was stopped by an old woman washing the step who asked him what his trouble was. The potential magnitude of the question caused Arthur to break down and he poured his heart out to the woman. He told her much of what he had been through during the war and when he was done, she took charge. She went in to see the doctor and after what seemed an age, she returned and told him the doctor would see him again.

When he re-entered the surgery, the doctor apologised and said he had not known Arthur had been in a prison camp and subjected to so much hardship. Arthur wondered where he thought he had spent the war weighing less than seven stone, but he said nothing and was grateful for the attention. He was prescribed an oral tonic and a paste to rub into his legs, both of which proved extremely effective.

Understandably, Arthur found it difficult to stay indoors during those early weeks and when a local councillor wanted to invite him to a forum at the local cinema, it took him a while to track Arthur down. He had grave reservations about attending a question-and-answer talk, but with the words of Maria in his thoughts that he should tell as many as he could about what he had seen, he decided to go.

Also invited was a paratrooper who had been at Arnhem. The councillor, a Mr Hilditch, asked the two men questions in turn. The audience applauded as the two men entered the stage, but as each of the paratrooper's answers were met with cheers and more applause, Arthur's descriptions of the horrors he had endured were met with an embarrassed, stony silence. When the talk was over, the audience crowded around the paratrooper, while Arthur left unnoticed by a side door. The night was an unmitigated disaster and he vowed he would not subject himself to such a trial again.

All of Arthur's possessions had been sold to a second-hand shop by his stepmother, but the most serious loss to Arthur was that of his fishing tackle. This was put right by Margaret's brother, Harold Cross, who supplied him with a new set of tackle and from fishing Arthur was able to experience some form of therapy.

While on leave, he received mail from the Army asking how much he felt he should be recompensed for the labour he had done while a prisoner of war with both the Italians and the Germans. Arthur suspected some ulterior motive in the question and spent days wondering how much he should claim. He had not done any work while a captive of the Italians, but in the end put in a claim for thirty pounds for the labour forced from him at Auschwitz. He had decided not to claim at all but the deduction of twenty-two pounds by the Army from his back pay, for failing to return home with his rifle and webbing equipment incensed him greatly. Did they really believe the Nazis would have allowed them to keep their rifles in the camp? When a cheque for that amount was returned to him, he would not have given the matter another thought had he not come across a former Auschwitz inmate. His friend was astounded at Arthur's paltry claim; he himself had claimed close to a thousand pounds and been paid without question.

When his leave was over, Arthur was recalled to Brighton and from there was sent to Hastings. This camp was made for 150 men, but 300 had been sent here. The error was quickly and efficiently corrected by selecting every alternate soldier to receive discharge and a pension, irrespective of physical

The approach to Auschwitz. As many as 65,000 Jewish prisoners would arrive at Auschwitz every day.

The gates of Auschwitz bearing the Nazi philosophy: *Arbeit Macht Frei* – Freedom Through Work.

The England E715 football team, Auschwitz. Spud Murphy is seated in the front row, extreme right, and camp leader Charlie Coward stands in the centre.

An Auschwitz concert party programme, kindly donated by Bill Lemin's daughter, Ann.

American soldiers cross the Siegfried Line into Germany. Spring, 1945.

The eight representatives at the Nuremburg War Crimes Trial. Charlie Coward stands fourth from left, Fred Davison stands third from right and the others include Charles Hill, Leonard Dales, Eric Doyle, Robert Ferris and Reginald Hartland.

Arthur and Olwen on their wedding day, 21 September 1946.

Arthur fulfilled his promise to Maria, to tell the world about the atrocities he witnessed at Auschwitz.

One of the crematoria at Birkenau, destroyed by the Germans. Arthur returned to Auschwitz with the BBC in June 1999.

condition. Not for the first time Arthur Dodd lost out when Lady Luck was the dealer. He spent two months at Hastings before being posted to Western Command nearer home at Chester. After two weeks he was sent to a German POW camp at Wolgerton near Nantwich. Finally, he was sent to Blakemere Hall, where German POWs made bread which Arthur delivered to Winsford for distribution countrywide. Here he met Olwen, a corporal in the ATS in charge of five girls. One particular day Arthur had offloaded the bread and invited the five females to the NAAFI in the town for a cup of tea. The enraged corporal was left to handle the bread herself. On his return, Olwen put Arthur on a charge! Smiling to himself and admiring her Welsh zeal, Arthur chipped in, 'I'm going to marry you!'

From Blakemere Hall, Arthur was demobbed and returned to civvy street and on 21 September 1946, Olwen became his bride and his strength through nigh-on forty years of nightmares.

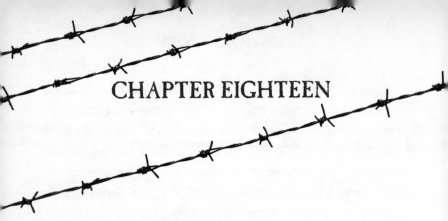

CHAPTER EIGHTEEN

Arthur Dodd does not underestimate the good fortune he enjoys in surviving the horrors of World War Two. At St Valery, Tobruk and on many occasions in Auschwitz, he did not believe he would survive. That he did, he credits to the love and compassion of God. Certainly, without his faith he could not have endured the trials of a concentration camp and would not have found the will to live.

He readily concedes that the treatment of the British POWs, as dreadful as it was, was infinitely better than that of the Jewish prisoners. His nightmare was not so much what he himself endured, but rather the inhuman brutality that he witnessed. All of his worst memories focus upon what he had to watch, not to what he himself was subjected.

Three weeks before the end of the millennium, Arthur was 80 years old. In the twilight of his life, there is nothing he enjoys more than gardening, fishing and bowling. He watches the constant uniformity of the seasons and wonders at the contrast of just how uncertain human life can be. During the war, he lost count of how many times he confronted death. How many people can say their life has flashed before them three times?

ARTHUR'S STORY

There are few gentiles who can testify to the barbarism of the concentration camps. The current argument of neo-fascists is that the Holocaust is a fiction or, at least, a gross exaggeration. Tell that to Arthur Dodd. He has no political axe to grind, no theological or genetic point to make. His story is simply an account of what he saw and it has taken him more than fifty years to tell it.

Even students of World War Two are generally unaware that British POWs were held captive at Auschwitz and there are now only a small number of them left. It was not until 1992 that they were first approached by the media. An article in *The Independent on Sunday* by Zoe Heller was based on brief interviews with three of the surviving British POWs, one of whom was Arthur. This represented the first time Arthur had publicly divulged many of his experiences at Auschwitz and he found Ms Heller's treatment of the subject both intelligent and sympathetic.

Film-maker Maurice Hatton became aware of the existence of British survivors of Auschwitz after reading Primo Levi's account of the camp in *If This is a Man* and put together the documentary *Satan at his Best*, a title suggested by Arthur himself. Levi was a trained chemist and had worked at the same Buna synthetic rubber plant, financed by I. G. Farben, as Arthur. The close proximity of a coal-mine, three rivers and an endless supply of slave labour made the location of Oswiecim a sound investment for the chemical industrialists, but it is to the credit of both the POWs and the partisans that not one ounce of synthetic rubber ever left the plant.

For more than three decades after the war, Arthur suffered badly from repetitive nightmares, migraines and other stress-related sicknesses. Many times, when his sleep was disturbed and peace would not come, he would pick up his Bible for spiritual sustenance. Once, in 1981, he opened it at random and began reading Hebrews 10: 32-35.

Don't ever forget those wonderful days when you first learned about Christ. Remember how you kept right on with the Lord, even though it meant terrible suffering. Sometimes you were laughed at and beaten, and sometimes you watched and sympathised with others suffering the same things. You suffered with those thrown into jail and you were actually joyful when all you owned was taken from you, knowing better things were awaiting you in heaven, things that would be yours forever. Do not let this happy trust in the Lord die away, no matter what happens. Remember your reward.

It was, however, not the Bible that proved to be the turning point for Arthur. Picking up a copy of *Reader's Digest*, he read an article by Jules Segal, a psychologist, who had treated the eighty American hostages held in Iran. Segal referred to a large number of World War Two veterans who had experienced nightmares for many years after their return to the US and stated that the most successful form of therapy had been for the survivors to talk openly about the memories that haunted them.

As luck would have it, Arthur was due to attend a meeting of the Methodist Fellowship the following night and he called the organiser, Roger Jones, and asked if those assembled could stay on for an extra half an hour or so, as he had something he would like to talk about. The experience in the cinema years earlier had left Arthur far from convinced that such therapy could work, but he was determined to see it through.

There were a dozen people seated around Arthur as he nervously began to tell his story. He described the brutal treatment and the murders, the skeletal frames, the stench of the dead and the dying. He told them about the gas chambers and the smoke, and the names of the German companies prepared to profit from the Holocaust. He told them about the man who traded the socks Arthur had given him for food, the young girl beaten at the side of the road, the children thrown onto roaring flames. He related how he had watched a group of young children being walked to the gas chambers and how, all these years later, he still cannot look at schoolchildren walking in crocodile formation without crying. Finally, after talking uninterrupted for nearly half an hour, he broke down and cried. Roger's wife, Glen, came over to him and put her arms around him. Roger brought the meeting to a close and after gathering himself together, Arthur went home. Mr Segal was right. From that night, Arthur's nightmares stopped. Auschwitz is still the first thing he thinks of every morning and he will be forever affected by it. But the awful nightmares and the punishing migraine attacks are behind him.

Two other Northwich lads survived Auschwitz, Tommy Dingham and Terry 'Spud' Murphy. Tommy was a very brave person, afraid of nobody, never losing his spirit and giving the Jerries no end of aggravation. He and his two mates were inseparable. 'Burnsie' was a neat and tidily dressed Scot and 'Simms' was a Yorkshireman. Tommy told Arthur of the night the three pals were under the German mess building. They could hear their camp leader, Charlie Coward, laughing and joking with the Nazis and drinking their beer. No doubt that was his way of fighting the war by gaining the confidence of their hosts. To others, however, his fraternising with the enemy brought anger and suspicion.

Arthur saw little of Tommy in the camp, but they became firm friends after the war. As tough as he was, he found it increasingly difficult to cope with the memories. He did not take Arthur's advice to talk openly about Auschwitz and refused to cooperate with the Maurice Hatton film. Like other British POW inmates of Auschwitz, witnessing indescribable horrors all around them daily for close on two years had a greater effect on Tommy as he grew older. A turning point occurred when he was in a Hartford residential home. One day acute depression and flashbacks caused a disturbance in his mind and he showed himself naked to three of the ladies in the home, and was subsequently sent back to his own home. After spending time in a mental institution, Tommy died on his own in a small bedsit in February 1994. Living with the sights and sounds proved too much for Tommy Dingham. Auschwitz had claimed him in the end, as sure as if he had been gassed and cremated. Only six mourners attended his funeral in St Helen's church in Northwich, Arthur among them, together with his son, Geoffrey. It was a sad and solemn occasion and he turned to Geoffrey, choked with emotion.

'He deserved better than this,' he said.

Arthur lost touch with 'Spud' Murphy on the march from Auschwitz and it was some time later before they discovered they were both Northwich lads and met up again. Spud was mentally tougher than most and came out of the camp probably as well as anyone. He was an excellent footballer and managed Barnton Football Club after the war. Sadly, he died of Bronchogenic Carcinoma on 28 May 1973. Arthur always saw Spud as a good, balanced family man of excellent character, an opinion that was echoed by his only daughter, Christine. 'Dad was a very calm and peaceful man who nevertheless never ever failed to mention to his children who dared leave any scraps of food on their plate, "I knew so many men who would kill for such leftovers". Those starving Jews of Auschwitz were never far from his thoughts and this kind man must obviously have tried to help those oppressed wretches because one of them gave him a ring exquisitely made from a nut which now proudly adorns the finger of my eldest brother.' Private Edward Murphy 3773306 of the 1st Battalion Kings Own Royal Regiment later became POW 221552 of Camp E715 Monowitz and a proud member of the Camp's England football team. 'Dad was in hospital on his return to England and always seemed to suffer from chest complaints for the rest of his life. He explained to Mum some of his horrific experiences whilst working near skeletal Jews at I. G. Farben but told her never to tell their children. This promise she duly kept to her dying day in 2002,' Christine added proudly.

Arthur Dodd has kept his sanity by reading his Bible every day. He was also assisted immeasurably in his slow recovery by his wife Olwen, with whom he had a son and a daughter. They in turn have given him six grandchildren and they are the source of much of the joy in his life today.

Arthur will never forget Auschwitz. But the memory of it now comes to him only in waking moments when he thinks back to an extraordinary episode of his life. He will forever be able to recall the most minute detail of what happened in Polish Silesia, but the nightmares have stopped. Finally, after many years of torment, Arthur has found freedom and with it some peace.

CHAPTER NINETEEN

It had always been Arthur's wish to meet again some of the lads with whom he shared both exciting and frightening moments in their constant policy of non-cooperation with their German hosts. Local journalism pulled out all the stops to discover some of the survivors who had been in contact with Arthur in his time at Auschwitz.

'Search For Heroic Men Of Auschwitz' ran the headline in Newcastle-on-Tyne's *Sunday Sun* on 6 December 1998. They were searching for two brave Geordies who, along with Arthur and two other Brits, had put their lives on the line for Jews and Poles they did not even know.

The *Liverpool Echo* dated 16 February 1999 carried the message, 'My Search for Survivor of the Holocaust'. The search was on for Shaw, the chirpy Scouser who worked with Arthur on the derrick, the collapse of which unfortunately killed a number of Jews that day.

'Yorkshire Search for Saint who Survived Auschwitz' was prominently shown in the *Yorkshire Post* of 18 June 1999. This time the subject was one of Arthur's personal heroes, Jim Purdy, known to have been an amateur football referee in Yorkshire after the war. Jim always insisted his lads never pose for photographs for the Germans lest they be used for propaganda purposes.

These three headlines, however, failed to come up with any leads at all. Those proud saboteurs of I. G. Farben's dream factory are now thin on the ground.

It was to be expected that the first publication of Arthur Dodd's story would in itself generate more information on the subject. In addition to the many letters that Arthur received, BBC Television stepped forward and offered to take him back to that bloodstained strip of Polish Silesia.

The publicity surrounding Arthur's story aroused the darkest corners of his memory long before his return to Poland. It was a dismal Wednesday afternoon in February 1999 and Arthur took to his bed for a lie down. With classical music in his headphones, he drifted into sleep. Not long after, he re-emerged, sobbing heavily. The music was vaguely familiar but he could not understand why he was so emotionally distraught. A couple of weeks later everything fell into place. The presenter of his favourite Classic FM programme had introduced Beethoven's *Egmont* Overture. It was that tune again, the one often heard during the daily Jewish selection process at Auschwitz… to work or to die. The classic rendition that had prompted Arthur's tears 54 years later was no less than the favourite of Dr Josef Mengele, the so-called 'Butcher of Auschwitz'.

Arthur had always been mystified as to why the series of warehouses containing the Nazis' stolen commodities were referred to as 'Canada'. An Auschwitz guide confided why each building, whether holding human hair, brushes, spectacles or suitcases, was dubbed with that seemingly inappropriate name. In the two or three years immediately preceding World War Two, numerous Poles from that part of Silesia had emigrated to Canada. Quite soon many of them were sending food parcels back home to family in Poland. Other Poles were very impressed that such sacrifices could be afforded so soon. Canada was thus viewed as a place of great worth, just like those warehouses that continually pumped aid back to Berlin to help the German war effort.

In the Auschwitz–Birkenau Museum, the contents of these warehouses are exhibited in huge glass-fronted showcases, approximately thirty feet long by nine feet wide. When one realises these voluminous collections are but the tiniest fraction of what was left when the Russians liberated the camp, the scale of this deadly 'solution' is mind-blowing. In the same room as the human hair collection, there is a roll of material recovered from Germany and made from Jewish hair for officer's clothes.

Another room displays many thousands of shoes, which, even under protective special lighting, are slowly being rendered more charcoal grey in colour. Here and there amongst the masses of foot apparel are the coloured high-heeled female type. Maroons and blues have retained their colour and help break up the depressive span of grey hues. Towards the front of the case is a two-year-old's little white shoe. In a room where no music is played and people are lost in silence with their own thoughts, this contrasting miniature seems to be crying out, 'Don't forget me, I was here!' This most moving instant makes holding back the tears extremely difficult.

It was the morning of Monday 28 June 1999 and a chill

ran up Arthur's spine as he gazed up at the Third Reich's hollow message to the multitudes of incoming Jews, *Arbeit Macht Frei*. He remembered the entrance, he remembered the SS beating too. He remembered so much. He could see his dear friend, Maria Kostka, pleading with him to tell the world what had happened there. Belatedly he had fulfilled that request, for he had come back with the BBC to make a documentary film. Hopefully hundreds of thousands and possibly even millions of people would obtain an insight into the dark, satanic secrets of evil Auschwitz.

All the memories returned to him. During the course of any working day he might move dead Jews from a passageway to a place of no hindrance. Even when he had reached his lowest weight of six stone ten pounds, lifting these skeletal carcasses was so easy. They were but weightless skin and bone.

Although fine detail can mist over, how could he forget the horrors and brutalities when, in June 1999 working with the film crew, sores on his legs were still clearly evident? These ugly reminders had appeared on and off for fifty-four years and still had not finished forming. Minute pieces of shrapnel, reminders of the tragic Gala Day bombing, were still working their way out of his body. Arthur expected his return to be traumatic and he was certainly proved right when, on four separate occasions in particular, his emotions got the better of him.

The first instance was in the Jewish block at Auschwitz at the execution wall, a bullet-riddled, reinforced brick construction joining two blocks of prisons and making it a killing cul-de-sac from which there was no escape. The thing that got to Arthur in this instance was the maximisation of cruelty, which, in the case of the Jews, knew no limits. The windows of one of the blocks were shuttered but the others were not, allowing the family of the condemned, including their children, to witness the taking of their loved one's life.

The next location was the site of the air-raid shelter in Camp VI, an image he has always struggled to come to terms with. Paying homage at this mere dent in the ground, Arthur could almost feel the irritating brick dust at the back of his throat and hear the screams for any miners to come forward to assist. Gala Day was a day to which everyone had looked forward to with relish, buoyed by the continuing good news of the war after D-Day. They had all worked hard using enterprising ideas; the spirit had been infectious. His tears welled up as he thought of those brave lads whose lives were taken by a bomb from their own side. The surviving of earlier sufferings served only to rub salt in the wound of their passing.

Whilst in the punishment block in Auschwitz, the lengths to which the Nazis would go to bring degradation to the Jews was brought home to Arthur with a vengeance. He thought he had seen it all, but looking at the 'standing cell' was too inhuman to comprehend. It was a bricked square, three feet by three feet and, due to demolition, was currently only about two to three feet high. In one side there was a very low door that the four men, one at a time, had to squeeze into on their belly. The four wretches could just fit in the standing position tightly packed. When in use, the height of the cell would be approximately seven feet. Arthur had witnessed for 22 months the constant beatings of Jews with club and whip. When these were administered by a kapo, the SS received immense pleasure seeing Jew ill-treat Jew. Imagine, after a 12 day of degradation and humiliation, to then have to spend all night in the 'standing cell'. Depending on what the Jew was supposed to have done or not to have done, the term of the punishment would be between three and seven nights. The thought of their pain-racked, skeletal frames so tightly packed together with the obvious discomfort from bodily functions proved too much for Arthur to take.

The fourth and last location that caused Arthur acute emotional stress was one of the women's huts at Birkenau. Each layer of the double-tiered beds in any normal society would hold two people. Birkenau was far from normal. Never were there less than six women in each layer. In the latter part of 1944 when the rate of elimination of Hungarian Jews reached fever pitch, no fewer than fifteen women were packed into that same restricted space. Pre-war, the women's huts were originally stables for a Polish cavalry unit. Each hut had an oven with a brick casing to take heat along the length of the building in order to maximise the comfort for the horses. To the Nazis, Jews were never considered as important as horses. Never were these ovens lit for the Jews during the course of the war, even during the bleakest of winter temperatures. The lack of privacy, the lice, the bugs and the cold meant for these women death must have been viewed as a blessing.

ARTHUR'S STORY

Arthur's return to Auschwitz was nearing its end and the desire closest to his heart still had not been fulfilled. Despite much appreciated assistance from the curator of the State Museum of Auschwitz–Birkenau, he still could not embrace that proud patriot and dear friend, Maria Kostka.

Diligent searching in the archives of the Museum as well as in the local County Office for evidence of people in Oswiecim revealed there were two females of that name, one born in 1916 and the other in 1925. Arthur considered, after much thought, that Maria was slightly older than he, suggesting the former female. Both girls, however, left the town after the war and could not be traced.

Success was more forthcoming when consolidating the positions of Arthur's two camps of residence, E711 and E715. From the description of the comparative luxuries of E711, its only possible location was in the grounds of the so-called *Lehrlingsheim* (or *Jugendwohnheim*) that was situated about 300 metres west from Monowitz Camp VIII. The purpose of setting up the *Lehrlingsheim* was to provide quarters for young ethnic Germans from Silesia who were to be educated in chemistry in order to create a managing core for the future staffing of the factory. The youths were submitted to intensive ideological indoctrination according to patterns developed by the Nazi Youth Organisation (the *Hitler Jungend*).

Unbeknown to Arthur, British POWs were housed in three different camps in the Monowitz complex. The camps were some distance apart and, with different groups working in different areas of the factory, individuals could be excused for thinking they were in the only camp holding British POWs. Most of Monowitz has been totally destroyed and each camp comprises green pastures with occasional basic pointers to earlier positions of walls and gateposts.

Arthur was first shown Camp VIII, known to the Germans as *Karpfenteich*, located near a big fish pond on its eastern side, about 500 metres south from the factory. He received no vibes of recognition and shook his head in frustration at the lack of confirmatory evidence.

Camp IV provided a similarly disappointing result. After the war, local farmers and smallholders stripped the wooden buildings from the camps and built new serviceable amenities. Just yards from a smart memorial to all races who lost their lives at Monowitz, upon which Arthur placed some flowers, stood a small, very ordinary-looking wooden stable. Its weathered laths aroused deep feelings in Arthur.

'I could have slept in you,' Arthur murmured as he stroked the special timber, special because it is the only remaining section of wood still in use today that originated from the Monowitz British POW camps.

By the time Camp VI was in sight the atmosphere was tinged with anxiety in the researchers' desperate search for confirmatory evidence that this was indeed the land on which he had spent those twenty-two months of horror. Arthur was first off the minibus, the rest of the group allowing him space and privacy to explore. He busied himself like a bloodhound in numerous directions before beckoning the rest over.

'I really think this could be Camp E715 as I knew it,' he exclaimed, his eyes dancing with anticipation. Keeping by the roadside he pointed out where the hospital had been and, yards away, the hut where the Gala Day pantomime was destined to take place prior to the arrival of the American bomb. Going back to the road, which was a mere cart track in the years 1943–45, in the direction away from the factory, he became quite excited as he identified a depression in the ground corresponding to the approximate position of the air-raid shelter that took that direct hit on Gala Day. Finally, for Arthur, the conclusive landmark was the still-intact one-man bunker near the roadside. This was solely for the use of the Wehrmacht sentry during an air-raid.

Someone pointed to the small farmhouse situated about eighty yards in from the roadside. An elderly man answered the door and was confronted by an excited Arthur Dodd, eager to confirm his suspicions.

'English POWs here,' he exclaimed, pointing to the ground. The old man unfortunately knew no English and, with a shrug of the shoulders, turned back to call to the house. A little old lady then appeared and Arthur repeated his question. Even before she could answer, Arthur knew from her eyes that she understood.

'English here, *ja*! *Ja*!' Stefania Wactawek cried. It was indeed an emotional moment for the Cheshire man: he had returned.

The curator of the Auschwitz Museum conversed with her in Polish and it transpired that, as a youth, she lived in a village two to three miles away and passed Camp VI daily en route to her job in one of the canteens in the I. G. Farben complex. She smiled when recalling some Saturday nights in a hut near the perimeter wire, which on occasions could loosely be viewed as a recreational centre. She remembered the English soldiers and their dark home-made beer and the fun times she and other local Polish girls enjoyed. Such evenings were only possible if the guards on duty succumbed to a bribe. Of the some twelve to fourteen custodians, two-thirds of them would look the other way for cigarettes or chocolate. Arthur never frequented this building at night due to his looking after the mentally disturbed Alan Blades.

As he walked over the now empty plot, he could place this 'recreation hut' alongside the now busy road, next to which was the Camp Leader's hut and, on the other side of the main entrance, the hospital and the British air-raid shelter where the Gala Day tragedy took place. Arthur's own hut was at the end of the camp furthest away from the road, grass now covering the nine-foot square latrine that had been placed outside, no doubt still retaining the bones of the German informer.

Camp E711 was a good two kilometres from the factory but E715 (Camp VI) was mere yards away. He could see clearly the men forming up and turning left out of the gate, proceeding between 100 and 150 yards to the first entrance to the I. G. Farben Works. At this point about twenty of the men peeled off, including Charlie Piddock from Southampton, Shaw from Liverpool and Arthur. Arthur and Charlie went directly to Building BAU 38, with the Scouser working in an adjacent area. The rest of the detachment was distributed through numerous other entrances further on down what was then a dirt track.

Until his return to Auschwitz, Arthur had laboured under the false assumption that the camp he was in was the only one housing British POWs within its fenced boundaries. Consequently his estimated numbers of that category of prisoner were below the true figure, as Camps IV and VIII had never come into his calculations. The maximum number of British POWs employed on the construction site for I. G. Farben reached 1,150 between October 1943 and the end of that year. The official figures obtained from the archives office showed that figure plummeted dramatically in mid-January 1944 to 500, recovering in early February 1944 to about 925. Other documents show that between March and May 1944 the number of British prisoners in Monowitz gradually declined, from 693 to 660; in October that year they numbered 577 whilst in January 1945 only 574 remained.

Good cooperation from the curator of the Auschwitz–Birkenau Museum produced evidence of the German opinion of the attitude of the British POWs in and around the factory. The weekly reports for weeks commencing 18 October 1943 and 25 October 1943 from the I. G. Farben plant at Oswiecim, expressed by Chief Engineer Maximillian Faust, centres on the low work efficiency of the British POWs. He writes:

'There are very few guards at our disposal and, being of such a low moral standard, consequently are unable to extort any discipline from their inferiors and maintain the required speed of work. To make matters worse, the British prisoners are being lavished with gifts from their Red Cross parcels.

They are distributing cigarettes and chocolate to Poles and concentration camp inmates and probably also to their guards. The English are adopting a quarrelsome attitude and, despite being directed to work in large numbers, their productivity is well below the average.'

I. G. Farben planned to enter upon a production of synthetic rubber in January 1945 and to reach its full capacity in the autumn of that year. Before the beginning of the air strikes in August 1944, the factory was able to produce about 3,000 tons of methanol per month together with small amounts of tar, heavy oil and gasoline. No doubt the failure to produce synthetic rubber was due in no small measure to the non-cooperation of the British prisoners.

The Polish partisans trusted nobody but the British POWs to assist them in their fight against the Nazis. To anyone having seen the 22 film made by the Red Army when they liberated Auschwitz, it seems unbelievable that only one country is omitted by the authorities at Auschwitz from the huge list of countries of origin of all those killed at Auschwitz–Birkenau. That country is Great Britain.

The most uplifting moment of Arthur's momentous return to Auschwitz came when he suddenly became aware of scores of swallows, chattering loudly as they swooped like Spitfires from the skies. After the total absence of bird life over that death camp during the years 1943–45, they represented a symbol of victory. Good had triumphed over evil.

PART TWO:
OTHER ACCOUNTS

Jewish victims who suffered such atrocities and the unfortunate POWs who found themselves witness to this appalling saga at Auschwitz deserve a voice. Many people discredited Arthur's story by refusing to believe in the presence of British POWs in Auschwitz. The accounts that follow from British soldiers and Jewish prisoners who contacted Arthur after the first edition of this book was published most certainly prove it was true.

Leon Greenman

Arthur heard many tales about a London Jew, camp number 98288, who repeatedly took risks to contact British POWs at Auschwitz. A few years ago Arthur discovered his story. Born in November 1910 in Artillery Lane in Whitechapel, London, Leon Greenman grew up in Holland where he trained to be a concert singer. His wife, Esther Van Dam, was born in Rotterdam, but they returned to England to marry in Stepney Green in 1935. They then went back to Holland, where their son, Barney, was born five years later. At the beginning of the war Leon was running an antiquarian book business and making regular trips to London.

The birth of his son was registered with the British Consulate in Rotterdam and it had been promised that the

Greenmans would be collected and taken to England when the Germans entered Holland. It never happened. When the Germans overran the country in May 1940, they were left behind. Leon handed his British passport and papers to a friend for safekeeping, but when he later asked for them, he was told they had been destroyed for fear of an accusation of collaborating with Jews. He then contacted the Swiss Consulate, but their request for new passports went unanswered. Because of Leon's Dutch grandfather, the family were registered as Dutch Jews by the police Chief Inspector responsible for aliens.

In October 1942, they were arrested and sent to the Westerbork camp in northern Holland and by January 1943 they were in Auschwitz. As he was marched away, he saw his wife and son being taken away on a truck. When he later asked a kapo what had happened to them, he answered by pointing to the sky. He never saw either of them again. Of the consignment of 750 Jews of both sexes and all ages, all but fifty were gassed immediately. Of the 50 put to work, Leon was one of only two who survived.

For two months in Auschwitz, he was engaged in a multitude of meaningless tasks, the objective being to break what little spirit the Jewish prisoners had left. He was once engaged in removing a mound of sand from one point to another by means of filling the pockets of his prison uniform. They endured rigorous physical exercise in freezing conditions, always accompanied by repeated beatings.

He was transferred to Camp I and regarded himself as fortunate he was not one of those taken to the gas chambers instead. It was around April 1943 that for the first time he saw the uniforms of the British soldiers interned at the camp. He was keen to speak to his fellow countrymen as often as he could, but the practice was seriously discouraged and could only be done by bribing one of the kapos. He would ask the POWs for cigarettes, with which he could make a trade for soup slops from the kitchens. This was a hazardous business, but played a major part in keeping Leon alive. In return for the cigarettes, he would sing for the soldiers who appreciated the talent of his trained voice. He would shout across to the men, keen to let them know he was English.

'Hello! I'm Leon! Leon the Londoner!'

Leon never gave up hope that his incarceration would finally be seen as a mistake and he was keen to maintain what contact he could with the POWs. He took great risks to do so and was once badly beaten by a kapo for it after being spotted by a guard of the SS. The food and accommodation for the Jews was deplorable beyond words and they quickly learned that *arbeit macht frei* meant you worked yourself to death and then you were free.

Many Jews were medical guinea pigs at Auschwitz and Leon was no exception. For some, the operations were disfiguring and fatal. Some women had their vaginas cut away; men had their testicles removed. Leon was operated on by an SS doctor, Horst Schumann. During his operation, Leon was able to cry out in English.

'They are hurting me now!' he shouted. Whether or not it was his using English, Leon does not know, but Schumann ordered the test to be stopped. Nevertheless, he was urinating blood for weeks afterwards.

After his release, Leon learned that the papers confirming his British status had arrived at Westerbork only minutes after his departure. For the sake of less than an hour, he had lost his wife and son and suffered desperate inhumanities. On leaving the camp, he was marched to Gleiwitz with feet so swollen he could barely walk. On arrival at Buchenwald he was admitted to hospital. If not for his insisting he was suffering with nothing more than chilblains, the doctors there would have amputated his feet. He was in hospital until April 1945 and never complained about his feet. He knew that if the doctors inspected them he would lose them.

It was on 11 April 1945 that Buchenwald was liberated by the Americans and Leon was flown to Paris. He had spent no less than two years in Auschwitz. At the hospital there he was told that one of his toes had turned gangrenous and had to be amputated; it was a small price to pay, and Leon thanked God that the operation had not taken place while in captivity. In October he was reunited with his father and stepmother in Rotterdam and the following month he arrived in London. There he was met by his two brothers, recently demobbed from the British Army.

Leon vowed that if ever he escaped with his life from Auschwitz, he would dedicate the rest of it to letting people know of the horror of the camps. This he has done. He now lectures on the Holocaust all over the world, speaking out against fascism and racism, ensuring that younger generations know what happened. For this, Leon is subject to threats and abuse from neo-fascist organisations such as Combat 18, but he will not stop. He is as dedicated today in his fight against fascism as he was fifty years ago.

For his defiant enlightenment of today's youth, he was presented with the Order of the British Empire in the 1998 New Year's Honours list.

Norbert Wollheim

Another Jewish account not dissimilar to that of Leon Greenman revealed Norbert Wollheim, his wife and 3 year old son being arrested by the SS on 8 March 1943 during the last big anti-Jewish action in Berlin. On arrival at the station at Auschwitz, Wollheim was separated from his wife and son and never saw them again. That particular transport from Berlin consisted of about one thousand people but only 220, mostly young men capable of working and including Wollheim, were sent to the concentration camp Monowitz in trucks. His prisoner number was 107984. He soon came to the group nicknamed 'murder command 4' whose task it was to unload cement bags or constructional steel from the arriving freight cars all day long at a suicidal running pace. Prisoners who broke down were beaten by the I. G. foremen as well as the kapos until they either resumed their work or were left there dead. Norbert witnessed many such deaths and, in his first few days there, saw a Dutch Jew commit suicide by throwing himself in front of a moving train.

He noticed repeatedly, particularly during the time when the SS accompanied the labour unit, that the I. G. foremen tried to surpass the SS in brutalities. In addition these same I. G. personnel incited the kapos to take the good shoes from the new arrivals and keep them for themselves. It was also a rule that the inmates had no working safeguards, for example iron and steel had to be moved without the proper leather glove protection. Wollheim remembers well the I. G. foremen, even on days well below freezing, making the kapos order the prisoners to take off their coat, if they indeed had one, in order to speed up the work rate. From the summer of 1943 he was sent to a skilled labour unit as a welder and he soon realized that prisoners were always given the dirtiest and most dangerous tasks with little if any protective equipment supplied. Norbert worked for months without welding goggles and, whilst the prisoners who were E-welders did not get any milk at all, their German counterparts received milk on a regular basis. The I. G. foremen and Inspectors knew all about the care imbalances in the factory but the inspectors were the people the Jews feared most because they were known to be fanatical Nazis who used every occasion of unsatisfactory work to make a report to the office of the SS Command, Scharfuehrer Rackers.

Wollheim discovered from the British POWs through surreptitious chats that most of them were skilled workers by trade and had been assigned to the armament plant Buna against their will and consequently in violation of the Geneva Convention. Norbert's relation with the British lads became closer and his excellent English and German enabled news and information to be exchanged on a regular basis. That way the POWs were able to keep Norbert informed daily of the BBC news from London, for they had a secret receiving set in their barracks, and the German Jew, for his part, translated for the British the German army news bulletins.

Norbert Wollheim stated that Duerrfeld was the man who caused orders to be given to the German foremen to drive the concentration camp prisoners to the greatest possible work output. In these orders the German foremen were directly asked to make a report at once to the SS Kommandantura if they observed any case of idleness or negligence of work. Duerrfeld knew only too well that such reports would mean the severest punishment, even death, for the prisoner concerned.

Terry Gorman

Mike Gorman contacted Arthur in 1999 to tell him about his late father, Terry Gorman of the 5th Battalion Green Howards, of whom he spoke with pride and sadness. Terry was in a different camp to Arthur Dodd although, without realising it, the two had met briefly when Terry was on a makeshift operating table in the Farasabrina camp in Italy. His crude scar bore testament to the absence of medical instruments on that occasion.

The Green Howard had more than one job at Auschwitz, including the supply of firebricks from Auschwitz to the Birkenau crematoria. Arthur remembers seeing firebricks stacked up outside the technical *lager* where his Maria worked.

A New Zealand soldier helped Terry in this job; the two having front row views of the arrival of rail cattle trucks crammed full with their doomed cargo. Most Holocaust films show the sliding doors being opened immediately and the hapless Jews being driven unmercifully to meet their maker. In practice this did not always happen. Terry Gorman saw these rail transporters left locked up and suffered the mental torture of hearing the heart rending screams of the inmates and the sickening sight of their urine dripping from closed doors.

Terry and his New Zealand workmate would become familiar to the guards, who occasionally in winter months would let them warm their hands at the brazier situated just inside the main gatehouse.

Terry Gorman's main job at Auschwitz was in the boiler house or *kesselhaus* and, since temperatures encountered were so high, the POWs were allowed the privilege of a shower. One particular day he was showering with two others when the Germans suddenly shoved three Jewesses into the cubicle and left quickly. The women were stark naked and of skeletal form. There was acute embarrassment on both sides. Was this some sort of perverse humour from the Nazis? Were they spying from afar? The Germans came back for their charges but nothing happened, for nobody was thinking in sexual terms in such circumstances.

Stan Fawcett and Jack Walker were the other two Green Howards who shared the same camp with Terry, whilst Company Sergeant Harold Bagshaw looked after the needs of his men as Jim Purdy did for Arthur and the others in Camp VI. Charlie Murphy was in the same Battalion as Terry and the two were together at Lamsdorf. From there Charlie went to work in a coal-mine about twenty-five kilometres from Auschwitz but the two pals met up again on the march and he was Terry's best man at his wedding in 1946.

Yet two other Green Howards, Jimmy Davidson, who played the trumpet at Terry's wedding, and Ginger Parry were transferred from Camp IV Auschwitz to E393 Mittel-Laziek in January 1944 as shown in archive documents at Auschwitz.

Terry Gorman, as with many of the other Brits, suffered from post-traumatic stress and became very withdrawn in later life. The mention of Ginger Parry brought to mind an occasion that affected Terry very significantly. In the late forties the two met at Manchester's Central Station when Terry recognised with some difficulty the man begging from rail commuters. If it had not been for Parry's flaming red hair he would never have stopped. This once proud British soldier had fallen on hard times and was living in a cave in the Newton Heath area of the city. Terry took him for something to eat and drink but the pathetic sight of this tramp hit him hard. Realising all Ginger had gone through and seeing him like this was depressingly sad.

Tony recalled another terrible incident involving a South African by the name of Silver who slept in the bunk above Terry. One day there was an impromptu search by the SS. 'You are not Silver, you are Silverstein, you are a Jew!' screamed one of the SS officers. Despite the South African's earnest pleas to the contrary, he was shot where he stood. In this nightmarish way the SS enjoyed making examples of people. Little wonder that some of the witnesses lost their sanity. This incident reinforced the fact that anything could happen at any time in that hell-hole.

Fred Davison

Arthur heard in 1998 from Fred Davison Junior about his father, Fred Senior, who died aged only 46 when Fred Junior was just 12 years old. Young Fred thus learnt nothing about Auschwitz from his father, relying only on his mother's reconstruction of her husband's memories.

Fred, from Sunderland, enrolled in the Royal Army Ordnance Corps which was later embodied into the RASC. He was also captured at Tobruk and, like Arthur Dodd when asked his profession, answered in a comical manner. 'Brothel keeper's assistant,' was his mocking answer to his Italian host's question.

Fred remembered the day when the Germans tied the prisoners' wrists together because they claimed they had heard what was happening to German POWs in England. The British drove the guards crazy by each in turn continually asking for the toilet. Their hosts soon became exasperated, tying and untying their ropes. Wrists were bound by rope in the morning but by afternoon this was replaced by barbed wire and relations became decidedly ugly. The incident only lasted one full day but any fragments of good will that may have previously existed soured dramatically.

Fred and others worked under camp leader Sergeant-Major Charlie Coward in the marshalling yards, sending goods trains to the wrong destinations whilst sand and gravel replaced lubrication on moving parts. The resultant mayhem had an adverse effect on the German war machine and repercussions were serious. Their success, although good for morale, came at a high price with severe food restrictions. Fred and some mates resorted in desperation to eating dog. After the war he would never eat rabbit, claiming that it tasted too much like dog.

When Fred Davison and his group were first told they were going to Auschwitz they were instructed that they would be working for I. G. Farben in their paint factory. They soon realized they were functioning in a synthetic chemical complex. Camp Leader Charlie Coward protested that this was war work which prisoners did not have to perform. A dangerous situation was beginning to develop when the German Commandant smashed his fist on the table and, pointing to his revolver said, 'This is my Geneva Convention.' The sinister tone of his statement left no room for negotiation.

The I. G. Farben factory was a daily scene of noise, great activity, abuse and beatings, but nevertheless it became distinctly personal on occasions. Like other POWs Fred Davison became friendly in particular with two Jews, one Dutch and the other Greek, through furtive whispers as he carefully slipped them pathetic scraps of food. One day the Greek did not show up for work and his Dutch colleague pointed to the sky muttering, 'caput... smoke'. Davison inwardly was not surprised because only the previous week Streuber, the Farben Supervisor, had watched and commented on the Greek's work performance and could see that the man could hardly stand on his feet.

It was common everyday knowledge that the gas chambers existed; all the civilian meisters (a kind of departmental head) in the factory knew about it and, indeed, it was not unusual for the Farben foremen, meisters and supervisors to threaten the inmates that if they didn't work harder they would be sent to the gas chambers. Some of the Farben officials that Fred Davison knew personally had knowledge of the gassings. These included supervisors Bertram, a rough fellow who liked to use his revolver all the time, Kratsch, Weiss and Streuber. All were Nazis and all carried revolvers.

Nearly three years after cessation of hostilities Davison was astounded to receive a letter from Kurt Streuber dated 11 March 1948. In it the arrogant former Farben supervisor indicated that he was now a chief guard for the police in his home town of Bad-Kosen. His opening line was, 'My dear friend Fred, you will be astonished to get some sign of life from your workmates from Auschwitz.' One would never have guessed they were on opposite sides and that Davison had often risked a beating feeding scraps of food to the Jews Streuber chastised. The letter continued, 'We have got over the war well here and I hope that you also dear Fred have got over everything.' It transpired that Streuber had given some information to a visitor from London and had asked him to try to get this letter to Fred's address in Sunderland. Needless to say, this message was deemed in bad taste and did not warrant a reply.

Fred Davison attempted to explain to his son the pathetic state of the Jews, stating that he had personally witnessed, in his own work area alone, five members of this accursed nation dying daily from the winter cold. They often were forced to carry hundredweight bags of cement and, so weak were they, it would take four of them to put the bag on the back of one of their colleagues. If the inmate couldn't carry it or couldn't go along quickly enough to satisfy the meister, he would beat the wretches with clubs or iron bars until mercifully death came. Fred saw numerous lives eliminated in this most barbaric manner.

Fred Senior had never lifted a finger to his son but in 1965 when Fred Junior was 12 years old, a swastika was brought into the house from school. His father snapped at the sight of this insignia of evil, and internal emotional stresses born during 1943–45 in Polish Silesia exploded into a beating.

Only eight men represented the 1,100 or so British inhabitants of Auschwitz at the Nuremburg War Crimes Trial in 1947, two of whom were Sergeant-Major Charlie Coward and Fred Davison RASC. Five of the other six British POWs called to Nuremberg in July 1947 were Charles Hill, Leonard Dales, Eric Doyle, Robert Ferris and Reginald Hartland.

In Davison's Nuremburg cross examination Mr Minskoff represented the prosecution of I. G. Farben and Mr Hoffman its defence. Minskoff's opening question to Davison was to ask him whether he had ever been a member of the Communist party. The emphatic negative answer told the defence that the POW had no particular Russian sympathies.

Hoffman then proceeded to engage Davison in a contentious issue involving the unloading of 100 pound sacks of cement. In response to hostile defence questioning, the POW described accurately the location where he had seen often the onerous offloading operation, from the railway line at the bottom of E Street in the Auschwitz camp. The cement bags were also delivered by trucks. To the question of how far the inmates had to carry their heavy loads, Davison replied fifty yards or maybe more, and the time taken for a single journey between fifteen and thirty minutes.

Another controversial sight Davison had sworn to witness on four or five occasions was the beating to death with iron bars of the skeletal Jews. When asked the dates of these sightings, the Sunderland POW answered with December 1943, and then again in March, October, November and December 1944. Answers to additional questions revealed that on three occasions the SS were responsible and the other two were German civilian Meisters. Hoffman countered with a statement that there were hundreds of companies in Auschwitz and these perpetrators could have belonged to one of those. The Brit calmly stated, 'My own Meister's orders were all headed "I. G. Farben".' When asked whether he ever asked about names, Fred Davison added, 'It wasn't healthy to inquire about anything in that factory.'

John Green

In 1940, John Green of Warrington became POW 20220 in Stalag 20A at Thorn in Poland. The Germans decided they would educate the British by printing in English *Mein Kampf*, Hitler's autobiography, and distributing copies throughout the British community. One bitter winter's day with the temperature hovering as low as twenty degrees below, John decided it was too cold to go to work. He was consequently roughed up by two of the guards and hauled before the Commandant to explain his non-compliance.

'But I was reading *Mein Kampf*,' was his quick-thinking reply. He was excused work detail and sent back to continue studying the Nazi bestseller. The following day saw numerous Brits failing to appear in the workplace... all reading *Mein Kampf*, of course!

The man from Warrington had an early experience of Nazi arrogance and inhuman behaviour whilst watching skeletal Jews painfully struggle to make a series of square columns of reinforced concrete which were to support a large roof. Numerous stripees would negotiate mini-slopes that zig-zagged to ever higher levels, giving access to the edge of the pit. Each Jew would have to make superhuman calls on his diminishing strength pushing a wheelbarrow laden with concrete up one slope before handing over to the next prisoner. Consequently each slave would ascend higher and higher until reaching the 50 foot level where a particularly sadistic SS guard was in charge of the tipping of the concrete onto the rising column below. John Green witnessed the sad demise of a particularly exhausted inmate who very slowly just managed to tip his load with his very last dregs of energy. The SS guard screamed at the pitiful skin and bone frame to speed up and, once the pour had completed, accompanied with more expletives and deep disdain, the brute kicked the prisoner in the small of the back to his death 50 feet below. A POW from the white rose county and known as Yorkie to the lads had also seen the horrific humiliation and taking of life and whispered in his foreman's ear, 'He's dead John, take my word for it, he's dead.' The venom in his voice could not be missed. Three or four days later that same Yorkshire man asked John to cover him while he went to the toilet. Exchanging his tunic for a Jew's uniform he made his way up to the highest level with his wheelbarrow of concrete. With the element of surprise on his side, he pushed the SS scumbag off the platform into the liquid concrete below, closely followed by his own barrowful. Due to the noise of the busy workplace and the fact that German guards were totally occupied goading the multitudes of skeletal Jews, the brave act of atonement went unnoticed by the authorities. John Green reasoned with Yorkie that when the Germans later removed the shuttering around the concrete, authorities might indeed see evidence of the SS brute. 'I guess he must have slipped,' was the simple reply from the exacter of one of the sweetest acts of revenge.

John Green was an engineer, with 25 other Brits under him, from the same camp as Arthur Dodd, E715. John worked in BAU 921 on the production of methanol. A Royal Artilleryman, he had experienced a long internment, having been captured at Dunkirk. He remembers clearly his extremely short daily excursion to his workplace. Left out of E715, approximately one hundred yards up the road before turning right into the main entrance of I. G. Farben. After taking the first left past the main offices he was soon at BAU 921, nicknamed the *Queen Mary*, its three tall chimneys resembling in outline the famous liner.

John and his team worked on filtration systems, liaising with Hans Meyer, a Jewish architect from Brussels, all under the watchful eye of Meister Legel, the 60-year-old site engineer from Nuremburg. Stefan Zok was another member of management in that location, being in charge of civilian 'Gummy *Deutsche*' welders: Poles from the Polish/German border who would be rubber-stamped '*Deutsche*'. Another temporary member of staff, staying about three months, was Hitler Youth Herr Klinkie; aged between seventeen and eighteen, he was the epitome of the arrogant Nazi master race and certainly one of whom to be wary. Every occasion on his arrival at the workplace he would give a vigorous and exaggerated 'Heil Hitler!' To this Aryan showpiece John Green would give his equally vigorous one word response, 'Bollocks!' Meister Legel always returned the salutation with a half hearted response for not to return the Nazi salute from a fanatical party member meant great trouble.

The Germans were impressed with the skill of the British engineers, thereby making it easier for the POWs to engage in their own war against the Nazis: sabotage, a hindrance to the Third Reich that was nevertheless extremely dangerous. When assembling the tall filter tubes, the British lads would ensure the top few filters were secured properly whereas those lower down, usually beyond German inspection, remained loose. These 30 foot filter columns were dangerous objects to inspect from the inside, so the Germans rarely went very far down into them and this 'disciplined' sabotage represented little risk to the British POWs.

One unforgettable day whilst John was conversing with Legel, the site engineer received a visit from none other than

OTHER ACCOUNTS

Oskar Schindler, the German entrepreneur, endeavouring to sell I. G. Farben some of his Jewish-manufactured hardware. Meister Legel had told John Green an hour or so earlier to keep his lads working whilst this distinguished gentleman was in the vicinity. He also took a number of skilled Jews away from the areas Schindler was due to inspect, for Schindler was always looking to add to his complement of Jewish labour. Little did Legel know that the compassionate entrepreneur would enlist Jews whether skilled or non skilled in an attempt to save any of their miserable lives. The more Jews Schindler could get, the more he could save.

Although life in the factory was grim beyond comprehension, there were lighter moments and John remembers some of the characters who, for short periods, helped lift the ever enveloping gloom. There was Joe Deponio from Rhyl, a most entertaining mouth-organ player and Blanco White, a Royal West Kent from London. William Price-Williams from Rhudllan, north Wales, nicknamed 'The Cobbler', ran the cobbler's shop where he repaired both German and British footwear with an idiosyncratic style that indicated that he did something else in civvy street. The name Blanco White brought a wry smile to John's face as he recalled the time that procurement of radio parts was essential to maintain British morale as the war began to swing in their favour. The elderly guard assigned to BAU912, probably in his fifties, had a habit of nodding off occasionally and on one of these off guard moments Blanco surreptitiously stole a clip of ammunition from their minder. Ammunition was checked at the end of every shift and the imminent threat of the Eastern front or worse persuaded the old guy to find some radio valves for the British lads.

John himself kept busy by making all stage props for the Concert Party productions. The enemy enjoyed the British theatrical diversions. His greatest test was a request for a Wurlitzer organ capable of coming up from below floor level! It was a challenge that momentarily helped keep his mind off the horrors around him. He made an orchestra pit and lined the new pit floor using 'borrowed' German floorboards. Extensions were built on both sides of the organ to house numerous lights which were encased in white paper to give a Wurlitzer effect. Using a series of rollers and planks, at the start of the music the organ was lifted out of the pit – not unlike its more famous Blackpool counterpart.

John's more emotional memories include being in the burial party for the Gala Day victims and seeing signs of cannibalism on the death march. Man's will to survive was evident when he witnessed dead Jews in the snow with flesh hacked from the back of their legs.

Without a shadow of doubt the reason that many of the British contingency survived to attempt the death march home, albeit only just, was the supply of British and American Red Cross parcels. These heaven sent gifts included, amongst others, tins of McConnachie stew, tins of peas, cigarettes, tea, socks and scarfs and in Camp E715 on a trestle table, non smokers could swap cigarettes for food. John remembers how profitable the tea turned out to be, coming as it did in silver paper packets held in tins. After the tea had been used and enjoyed, the spent tea leaves would be dried and carefully repacked and sealed in the silver packets. These used tea leaves would then be exchanged with the Germans for pudding powder, a type of blancmange. The strange thing was the enemy actually enjoyed that second hand tea!

Douglas Bond

Douglas Bond 2364388 was 21 years of age when he joined the Royal Corps of Signals 56th Division in October 1939 and became POW 32851 when incarcerated in E715 as an unwilling employee of I. G. Farben.

Douglas remembers that when cigarettes were plentiful, which was not very often, he and his mates would barter with the civilians who worked for I. G. Farben for eggs and other long missed food delicacies. He remembered the spasmodic searching by the guards on returning to the camp from the factory. Winter supplied their best opportunities of smuggling their precious commodities past the guards. When wearing Great Coats they could make 'poacher's pockets' out of the linings and, when being searched, would spread open their coat with both hands. Nine times out of ten this ruse succeeded.

Like all his colleagues, Douglas greatly appreciated the lifeline of the Red Cross parcels. There may be more important things in life than food, but not to a POW. Where but in a POW camp would you find a fellow flogging his false teeth for a loaf of bread and then borrowing them back to eat it? Where else would a man sleep with a loaf under his neck, only to find on waking up some other hungry inmate had cut the ends off? Each Red Cross parcel weighed about ten pounds, most of this manna coming from England or Canada. When plentiful, the parcels would be shared between two or four prisoners but later on, when scarcity heightened, this number increased to six. Canadian parcels usually contained a tin of bully beef or spam, a packet of biscuits like Jacob's cream crackers but much thicker, butter, coffee, sugar, powdered milk called 'Klim' and a small bar of soap. English parcels were less lavish but offered an attraction in the variety of tinned meats, puddings and vegetables. Each group of POWs would decide on a weekly menu on receipt of a parcel, deciding how to stretch the food out over a week, but when the lads were really hungry the parcel did not last a single day. With cigarettes sent by wives or parents, again through the Red Cross, the inmates were able to barter with Germans or Poles in I. G. Farben for eggs, tins of pork and even Schnapps on occasions.

Douglas recalled a Sunday morning in late December 1944, their only day off in seven. 'From the top of my bunk I can just see through the window after scraping away the ice, it is around thirty degrees below outside with a couple of feet of snow on the ground. I see a German sentry, referred to as a Goon or sometimes a "Toadstool". In his sentry box he has on a top coat over which hangs his Great Coat, the whole lot must weigh a ton. The coat flares at the ankles which makes him look like a tent, and he is pegged down firmly with a pair of boots encompassed by an even larger pair of boots. He glares glumly through the wire, frozen, bored and cursing, he even envies us in our wooden huts. Being a Sunday we have a little laugh on him, here am I in bed with my Balaclava, Great Coat and mittens, my legs are swathed in old pants and stuck in a kitbag, only my clogs being removed. I am fairly warm! The hut is typical of all huts inside the cage, the asbestos lining on the walls is coated with ice and so is the roof, there are icicles on the few remaining beams with shirts and pants frozen stiff, some of which have been there for weeks. The camp has reached a low ebb, out of fags, out of Red Cross parcels, out of fuel and out of action. Some lie in bed too weak to stand, we just lie there all day, thinking of food, which we have not got. Not one of us speaks out loud on this subject as it causes arguments and fights. One thought only is in my mind, "please may I go home?"'

Cyril Quartermaine

Arthur always contested that the most traumatic element of being a POW at Auschwitz was witnessing at first hand the brutal and callous treatment of the Jews. In terms of physical effort though, the death march to the west was clearly the most stringent of tests. There were three British POW camps in Monowitz and therefore three different marches. Arthur Dodd's group from Camp VI walked all the way to Regensberg whereas a second group, Signalman I. H. Rolls', travelled by train. Cyril Quartermaine, who kept a diary of this time, represents the third group. The diary's minute size made it easier to hide from prying German eyes. Cyril, like Arthur Dodd, was in the RASC, his Army number, T151895 and his POW number, 222233.

The Russians took Auschwitz on 25 January 1945 but did not enter Cyril's camp, merely opening the gates to allow inmates outside. Unaware, Cyril continued working in the factory for two days. At midnight on 27 January he made a quick move out, grabbing two blankets and using bed boards to make sledges.

Arthur Dodd's column consisted almost entirely of British POWs from E715 whereas Cyril and his British colleagues were joined by Russians, Jews and Poles. Many Jews were quickly disposed of by rifles and grenades by the guards, and the smell of bodies was something that always remained with Cyril. They walked for three days before having a night's rest in a huge stable with many horses. Seven of them slept under five greatcoats and the blankets Cyril had managed to take from the camp. They bedded down in the horses' urinal trough enduring a temperature of minus thirty degrees. The march saw several casualties; a large number of men were lost simply from consuming contaminated grain stolen from a farm. The remainder of the march can be followed by Cyril's own diary entries.

Cyril's Diary

The roads are crammed with horse-drawn vehicles of evacuees as they pass through Jitchin, where police were lining the road in order to stop the people from giving the column food. The law officers were holding placards telling the people these POWs were gangsters who bomb their cities and children. It was here also that the Germans gave out leaflets asking for volunteers to join the German Army to fight the common fight against the Bolsheviks.

Arrive at Furstenbruch. All sledges have now been dumped. The people here are very good, giving us soup, pancakes and bread. I am billeted with twenty-seven men in a barn. Again well-fed with coffee and bread, home made cakes piled generously with jam and cooked potatoes.

Continue marching over ice and snowbound roads, passing dead Jews strewn along the roadside. Some are dead from cold and starvation, some shot or beaten to death. I got frostbite in the ears and they are swollen badly. Everyone very weak from lack of food.

Tuesday 13 February 1945
Passed over border into Czechoslovakia where reception is great. People rush out with carts full of cooked potatoes, bread and cakes, but our lads are so hungry they rush the people. Shots are fired. Saw our planes bombing with one being shot down in flames near Stanau.

Friday 16 February
Arrived at Lavice. Two thousand POWs billeted here. Guards and police stop the people giving us any food. Germans are mad to see us get food; people from surrounding areas with cakes, soap and big round 4 kg loaves, from which they'd slash off the slices with a great knife. Stopped Sunday here. Some lads wandered into the village and got bags of bread and were treated very well. One lad tried to leave in order to stay behind but was seen and shot.

Monday 19 February
Marched through Knezmost and Munchen Gratz and over the border into Germany. Again, the difference is noticed immediately as we arrive at Schiedel.

Thursday 22 February
The going had been horrendous as we arrived at Gross Priecen.

Saturday 24 February
We have had no rest this week.

Sunday 25 February
A rest day today for most of the lads are about all in with having no food. The MO manages to get a milk parcel for eight men from a local Stalag. Not much but it makes a drink.

Tuesday 27 February
Pass through Drux which has been bombed heavily.

Monday 5 March
Marched on through Gfell.

Tuesday 6 March
At Falken we are billeted in a brick factory unused for about two years. A terrible place, dirt and grime and no food. We stay here one day.

Thursday 8 March
Trudge on for the hungriest birthday I have ever had. Arrive at Klingen. The lads are dropping down like flies. Had half a mug of boiled swede.

Friday 9 March
Had a rest day today, just about all in.

Saturday 10 March
On the road we get a Red Cross parcel per three men. What an event, as we open ours and eat chocolate! Pass through Eger and reach Maulbach. Another parcel between two men which had not been issued on the road. They are American parcels but, on opening ours, we find it is bandages and medical materials.

Monday 12 March
We rest here. The parcels just save the boys, for we get no food from the Germans. When things were really bad, International Red Cross lorries appeared with food. They became known as the White Ladies, a descriptive term used to signify the lorries. They were driven by Canadian POWs, on parole from Stalag VIIA, still held by the Germans, who allowed them to undertake this task.

Tuesday 13 March
Had a bread issue from Jerry. We reach Thiersheim.

Wednesday 14 March

Continue to Roslau where we are billeted in a big factory. Very clean and we stop a day here. No food other than what's left of our parcels.

Friday 16 March

Arrived at Weissenstadt.

Saturday 17 March

Reached Gefree.

Tuesday 20 March

There was a rumour that this was to be the last day. We entrained and travelled first to Burneck and then to Bindlach near Bayreuth, seeing some of the great German *autobahn* roads.

Wednesday 21 March

Bread issue but very green and mouldy.

Thursday 22 March

Still hearing rumours of parcels.

Friday 23 to Tuesday 27 March

Remained at Bindlach and on the Thursday still had half an English parcel per man and some bulk biscuits and jam.

Wednesday 28 March
Rumour we were to move out at 4 a.m. but this did not transpire.

Thursday 29 March
Moved unexpectedly and received a parcel as we got on the train. Both English and American parcels were in the consignment. Open trucks pretty packed. Spend a night on the train.

Friday 30 March
Arrived at Nurnberg, which had been bombed all over. Moved into Stalag 13D, a very big place. Russians here as well. They are worse off than us and are in a hell of a state. Were deloused at 2 a.m.

Sunday 1 April
One parcel per two men in a compound with a great variety of nationalities. We had French NCOs in our tent.

Wednesday 4 April
Moved again at an unearthly hour, 5 a.m., to entrain to go we don't know where. The open wagons moved off around 10 a.m. Yankee planes over most of the time. Stood still for five hours after travelling about thirty kilometres. Something had happened for we went back, arriving in Stalag 13D around midnight in a different compound. Conditions not so good; no bed boards,

very little room and damp floors. Rumours circulated that the Yanks were near and that we'd be on the march again tomorrow.

Saturday 7 April
Still here. Yanks are said to be near. Our planes overhead pretty regular. Hell of a raid on Nurnberg yesterday. Ration very poor, no bread yesterday, no parcels in. We had one a man on Tuesday; that is the last they say.

Three more days at Nurnberg before we start night and day marching towards Munich. Passing blown-up tanks, dead men, horses etc. No bread, living on horsemeat. Fifty kilometres each day to walk, all in and just about had it. We intend to break first chance.

Monday 16 April
Getting machine-gunned by our own planes, hell of a feeling.

Saturday 21 April
Still marching, weather is warm now.

Tuesday 24 April
Refuse to go any further. Every man stands by the decision not to move.

Wednesday 25 April
We are evidently on a battlefield. Tanks, artillery etc. all here. We could be blown to hell at any minute.

Saturday 28 April
Twenty of us break from the column; all are going in groups. Guards are not bothered. We are near Moosburg.

Sunday 29 April
See tanks which turn out to be the Yanks. We have reached the front line. Contact them and find they are going to attack Moosburg. Go round to rear lines. We are free!

What is notable about the poignancy of Cyril's diary is the sheer number of times that he dwells upon food. Having been starved in the camps, the POWs found the search and attaining of food an obsession. Many British soldiers perished on the death marches due to malnutrition, disease, exhaustion and frostbite. Contending with these sufferings they could not keep up with the pace, dropping out to an inevitable death. But the numbers of the perished would have been very significantly higher, had it not been for the delivery of those vital Red Cross parcels. What may not be known to many is the part played by the Germans in this humane act.

The disheveled and forlorn rabble of men must have looked likely to accept any two bit deal from anybody in order to improve their miserable lot. Possibly that is why a certain turn of events happened that nobody could have foreseen. Germans handed out two pages of a typed letter addressed to 'Soldiers of the British Commonwealth and

Soldiers of the United States of America'. The document stated that the Moscow Kremlin sincerely believed the way was open for their conquest of the Western world. The events in the Baltic States, Poland, Hungary and Greece were proof enough for all to see the real programme behind the mask of Moscow's so called 'limited national aims'. It continued;

...it is not merely the destruction of Germany and the German race. The fate of Britain, the rest of Europe and eventually also the USA is also under threat. This means the fate of your wives, of your children, your home. It also means everything that makes life livable, lovable and honorable for you. We address ourselves to you regardless of your rank or your nationality. We think our fight has also become your fight. If there are some among you who are willing to join the ranks of the German soldiers who fight in this battle which will decide both the fate of Germany and the fate of your countries we should like to know it. We invite you to join our ranks. Whether you are willing to fight in the front line or in the service corps, we make you this solemn promise: whoever as a soldier of his own nation is willing to join the common front for the common cause, will be freed immediately after the victory of the present offensive and can return to his own country via Switzerland.

All that we have to ask from you is the word of a gentleman not to fight directly or indirectly for the cause of Bolshevik Communism as long as this war continues. At this moment we do not ask you to think of Germany.

We ask you to think about your own country, we ask you just to measure the chances which you and your people at home would have to exist in case the Bolshevik Communism onslaught should overpower Europe. Please inform the convoy officer of your decision and you will receive the privileges of our own men for we expect you to share their duty.

Make your decision now!

At the time Cyril Quartermaine did concede that some members of his multi national Death March group did disappear at that point, but whether they joined the Germans or simply left the column in order to make their own way home, he will never know.

Early in March 1945 a delegate of the International Red Cross visited a Canadian POW camp at Moosburg, and asked for twelve volunteers to drive trucks taking Red Cross supplies to prisoners on the move. There was an immediate response to the request, and on 8 March the volunteers were taken to Lubeck, where they met Paul de Blonay, a Swiss IRC delegate.

In the charge of Sergeant-Major Moss, the little party of twelve learnt that 50 loaded trucks were awaiting drivers at Constance, on the Swiss border. Then a further 30 Canadians and 22 Americans were recruited from camps at Lubeck, and eight men who had come to draw rations for liberated camps made up the number required.

When the men had given their word of honour that they would make no attempt to escape, the Germans allowed them to proceed by passenger train to Constance. There they found themselves in the German-held part of the town, with only a barrier separating them from Switzerland and freedom.

The drivers had plenty of opportunities to escape into Switzerland, but not one succumbed to the temptation. Had any done so, the Germans would have carried out their threat and taken every supply truck off the road.

Each convoy was accompanied by a German guard, but on a number of occasions some members of the SS tried to commandeer their cargo of food parcels and petrol. Thefts might have reached a serious level had not each driver been issued with a certificate by high-ranking officials of the Waffen SS. There were few occasions when these certificates failed to protect the Red Cross supplies.

The volunteer drivers received their freedom at Lubeck, on 2 May 1945 at 3.25 p.m., when the first British tank came rolling in. It was a great moment, but the work itself did not finish until 8 May. The convoy men remained in Germany for another six days feeding POWs and awaiting transport to the United Kingdom.

Mayer Hersch

Arthur Dodd met prisoner 138528 Mayer Hersh after the first edition of *Spectator in Hell* was published, during a locally organised Jewish evening. Arthur was deeply moved by what the former Auschwitz inmate had to say. Once the presentation had finished Arthur made his way forward towards the stage. Mayer looked the Cheshire man in the face as he approached. 'You were there weren't you?' gasped Mayer and the two embraced in tears.

OTHER ACCOUNTS

Mayer Hersh celebrated his thirteenth birthday on Thursday 31 August 1939, the last day of peace his native Poland was to enjoy for some considerable time. He came from Sieradz near Lodz in pre-war Western Poland, only 70–80 kilometres from the then German border. Even without a radio or a newspaper, word of the German invasion spread like wildfire. Friday was to have been the first day of a new term at the Jewish school but that establishment was never to reopen.

Including Mayer, the Hershes had six children. The family spent a short time with Mayer's great uncle in Zdunska Wola, for fear of the strategic town of Sieradz being totally destroyed. In those early days of occupation the Germans were totally ruthless, and, with planes bombing civilians and others being shot indiscriminately by ground troops, the demoralisation of the Polish people was complete.

The family returned home about a week later but times were hard for Jews as anti-Semitic feeling ran very high in Poland before, during and after the war. Going to and from school pre-war, Mayer was frequently chased and set upon by non-Jews. In the Polish population there was approximately forty per cent Jews and forty per cent *falsche Deutsche* and so the possibility of a Pole protecting a Jew was extremely remote. Severe brutalities against children of all ages were evident on the streets of Sieradz, and male adult religious Jews were subjected to having their bushy beards cut or burnt off with a cigarette lighter.

Mayer's elder brother, Jacob, was the first of the family to be taken for hard labour, but Mayer's turn was inevitably to come. In the middle of the night in March 1940, an armed German soldier and a policeman knocked on their door and called his name. He was taken from a warm bed at the tender age of 13 with his mother embracing him in floods of tears.

His first camp was Otoczno near Poznan where he stayed for about a year, assigned with many others to construct a new railway system and marshalling yards. The work was incredibly hard, leaving the camp at 5 a.m., work from 6 a.m. till 6 p.m., seven days a week. Their only food in 24 hours was four ounces of bread plus some clear, watery soup in which floated a little *kulraby*, a yellow vegetable only ever given to cows. Knowing there would be no food in the morning, young Hersh broke his bread into two, leaving one piece in his boot, which also served as a pillow. The following morning the bread had gone. It was a hard lesson to learn but learn he did, for he never left any bread again. The inmate's discomfort was compounded by no provision of beds, lying only on the hard floor. Due to boots often being stolen and the starvation levels of bread offered for a hard day's work, Mayer sold his footwear for a piece of bread.

As the railway pushed forward, so he was moved to his second camp at Lusenheim. Working on the railway some Jews were tempted to knock on the door of a nearby house and beg for food. Since the majority of homesteads were of Nazi sympathisers, this desperate decision represented extreme risk, for the Germans considered knocking on someone's door a direct attempt to escape. The penalty would be a terrible beating followed by death by hanging.

Mayer pointed out an unusual German rule to which they strictly adhered. If the Jew was under fourteen years of age, he would still receive a beating but would not be hanged. This most fortunate escape was afforded to a friend of Mayer's, who went on to survive the war. It was a strange German trait this, for they would beat or shoot to kill a 13-year-old, but never hang him.

Further down the line, his third camp was Guttenbrun, where Jews were dying like flies. Suicides were commonplace, the Jews leaving their move till the very last moment, throwing themselves in front of an oncoming train. Failed suicide attempts were to be avoided, for the German repercussions were worse than death.

In May 1943 16-year-old Mayer was one of very few survivors of the railway forced labour programme, and found that his reward was a one-way ticket to the most daunting camp of all, Auschwitz. Those Jews being transported had to give up all their clothing, which they were never to see again. In the naked form they were searched diligently in every orifice for jewellery and other valuables. Many Jews swallowed small precious items in order to reclaim them later. They were then kitted out with the blue and grey striped clothing, consisting of shirt, trousers, underpants, jacket and cap. The Nazis considered the cap important since they insisted the caps be removed in a gesture of deference whilst their owners were counted, and put on again once brought to attention after roll-call. It was just another small rule to put the Jews in their place, another mocking action to put a thin, satisfied smirk on an SS face.

Mayer was in Barrack 24 which, when full with one Jew per single bunk in the three-tier bedding, would house 1000 men. When the numbers increased dramatically, up to five Jews would share a single bunk. In a typical day for Jews in this death camp, they would be unceremoniously forced from their beds at 3.30 a.m. and inspected for roll-call at 4.30 a.m. and 7 p.m. Being counted twice a day left the weak, emaciated unfortunates little chance of escape but if someone did happen to escape the reprisals were brutal even by SS standards. One hundred hostages killed for one person missing on the count was not unusual. The working day was punctuated by frequent beatings with a whip or club in order to extract the last vestige of effort from skin and bone. As if that was not enough, on arrival back at the barracks the guards and kapos would viciously force them into line for their piece of bread and bowl of soup. Jews who had some experience of the practice would try to be at the front of the queue for bread when the slightly larger pieces were issued, but in the middle of the soup line-up, thereby avoiding the non-nourishing water from the top of the container.

Being young and agile, Mayer invariably found himself in the top bunk, whereas the older and more infirm could barely manage to crawl into the bottom bed. Gravity being what it is, the more obnoxious products from bodily functions always found their way to the lower layer. During the night the guards, just for sport, would wake everyone with their raging and screaming, beating many up, whilst the miserable creatures in the lower bunks would feel the full force of the

Nazi jackboot. Another favourite SS pleasure was to make the Jews practice a quick stand-to-attention in the early hours of the morning, when aching limbs were denied a night's sleep and the inmates slower to react would be given another vicious beating.

In the morning guards would be whipping them into the large latrine in the ground, whilst equally quickly another guard would be forcing them out. In attempting to avoid the blows, some Jews would slip into the stinking quagmire, from which, due to their weakened frames, they were unable to lift themselves out. Because of the sparse amounts of food available to them, a Jew would go properly to the toilet no more than once every five days.

People have several times confronted Mayer with the following question: 'When a large number of Jews were being controlled by possibly only two or three guards, why didn't they take the opportunity of taking these Germans with them?' Mayer has thought many times about this question and an associated one that derides the Jews for not fighting back and merely weakly accepting their fate.

Should a Jew have killed two Germans, a minimum of two hundred of their fellow Jews would be exterminated by shooting or hanging. In either case, their workmates would be made to parade in front of the dead in order to break their spirit still further. How could a man live with himself when he considered that some of those two hundred might have survived the atrocities of the camp had it not been for his hatred boiling over and leading to more wastage of human life? The other factor, that people who were not present at the carnage cannot appreciate, is just how weak the slaves became due to vastly depleted sources of strength and spirit.

In November 1944 a skeletal Mayer Hersh left Auschwitz, travelling to his fifth camp at Stutthof near Gdansk in northern Poland. Here, as in previous camps, Jews worked in close proximity to Russian POWs. As was the case in the German treatment of all undesirables, sadistic beatings with club, whip or leather belt were commonplace. However, the relationship between German and Russian was one of mutual distrust, hatred and fear. Mayer noted that a German, on beating a Russian unmercifully, always had a pistol in his other hand. The SS took no chances when dealing with the Soviet scum, as they always viewed them.

Camp number six was in Stuttgart in south-west Germany, arrived at after a long journey in cattle trucks of some 600 miles as the crow flies. On arrival, the 750 Jews were housed in a dilapidated aircraft hangar. Temperatures were well below freezing and snow filled their bunks. A few weeks later only 280 survived to trek to the seventh camp at Gotha, also in Germany. Here they were put up in underground bunks and engaged on loading and unloading ammunition, well-camouflaged from air attacks.

The Allies were extremely close by this stage and, in getting away in order to be of more use to the Third Reich, the Jews were made to run or be shot on the spot if unable to keep up. They had no food or water for twenty-four hours. They rested in an open field and slept. Many were shot overnight for no reason whatsoever. Next day Mayer and his very few remaining Jewish companions passed through a mountainous region to his eighth camp, Buchenwald, where they stayed for a week or less. Just three weeks later Jews and Russian POWs were loaded into open coal wagons and sent to Thersienstadt, a ghetto-cum-camp in Czechoslovakia, from where he was eventually liberated by the Russians.

A short man of light frame, Mayer Hersh had survived over five years of brutal hard labour. His weight on liberation, whilst still short of his nineteenth birthday, was just over four stone. He started out a naive thirteen-year-old but circumstances made him a man, in survival terms, by fourteen. After nine camps and sixty-two months of incomprehensible slavery, few could have matched Mayer's tenacity and will to live.

After the BBC documentary shown in September 2000 about Arthur Dodd, *Auschwitz – The Forgotten Witness*, several men contacted Arthur with their experiences.

Denis Avey
Denis Avey told of his time in E715, the same camp that Arthur Dodd endured. Originally enlisting with the Rifle Brigade, his Army number was 6914761 and eventual POW number 220543. Denis will never forget one dangerous but nevertheless humorous moment when, after a full day's work at I. G. Farben, the men were marched back to their camp and halted outside the wire, to be counted and searched yet again. Denis was standing next to a Cockney friend, Phil Hagen, when a thorough search of the Londoner revealed a scrawny

chicken, feathers and all, hidden between his legs inside his trousers! Immediately, as always, there was an abundance of shouting and threatening with guns. Denis, Hagen and the other chap were taken out of the line, beaten up and thrown into a bunker. As they spent a freezing night without food or water they pondered their fate. The following morning in the Hauptman's office they feared the worst as the question rang out, 'Where did you get this chicken?' Denis will never forget Hagen's classic retort, 'I was working very hard when this chicken attacked me and I had no option but to kill it in self-defence!' Then followed the silence of a lifetime for the three Brits before the Hauptman collapsed with laughter, the guards following suit seconds later. This turn of events saved the lads a long period of suffering in the bunker and possibly also the life of the Polish civilian who had supplied the chicken, for Denis is sure they would have found him had the enquiry proceeded.

Moments of humour were few and far between in this hell-hole, where inhumanities were on a scale friends and families would find impossible to appreciate. One brutality Denis witnessed that will remain with him forever was a female SS officer attempting to extract the last dregs of life from a male Jewish carcass. She punched the pathetic figure to the ground with her fist and, picking up a substantial rock, crashed it down on his head. This elimination of life from a tormented body was an everyday occurrence and these bestial acts, together with the memory of the repulsive stench of burning flesh, still bring depression and nausea to Denis Avey.

Since representing London schoolboys in 1931, soccer had always been a passion for Denis and playing for the South African team from Camp E715 was a great form of escape, albeit momentarily. There were too few South African soldiers to form a team and their numbers were supplemented by the English. The team went on to win the international tournament.

Whilst in Monowitz, Denis saw a copy of an SS Headquarters edict and subsequently managed to obtain a newspaper, the *Beobaelten Zeitung*, which reported this edict in detail. It read, 'When we achieve ultimate victory all British POWs will be executed. We shall invade England and all males aged between sixteen and sixty-five will be transported to Europe in order to rebuild the ruined cities. We shall exterminate all females over child bearing age. We shall govern the country from Whitehall and our victorious soldiers will be allowed to impregnate all suitable females with good Aryan blood.'

After the war Denis spent two years in hospital, a time punctuated with surgery for systemic tuberculosis in his lungs, throat and stomach. In addition, complications arising from a blow from a Luger pistol during his stay at Monowitz resulted in the loss of an eye. The incident leading up to this great personal loss occurred when Denis was working in a trench laying cables with Jews working in very close attendance. Suddenly a German guard started hitting a 'Stripee' with his rifle butt and kicked him viciously again and again. The prisoner was pitifully thin and was trying to stand to attention, his hat off, and not offering any resistance whatsoever. The blood was literally pouring down his face as Denis shouted at the guard to stop. An SS Officer came up behind the British POW with a Luger in his hand and hit Denis across the face, the gun's trigger guard catching his eye.

Like many other POWs, Denis is bitter because, despite the magnificent effort given to obtain victory and freedom for millions, these heroes were merely given a cheap demob suit, a woefully inadequate war pension, and were pitched into civilian life without counselling.

Auschwitz was absolute evil and it bred evil. There were no bees, nor butterflies nor flowers; it was as though nature had gone on strike. To Denis Avey it seemed the great architect of life had turned his back entirely on the whole place. On incarceration in this hell hole working for the German war effort, his philosophy was that of Oscar Wilde, 'stone walls do not a prison make, nor iron bars a cage'; he would quote this to his workmates and sabotage became their common focus. Coming from an engineering background Avey could recognise the Achilles heel of any equipment – no big bangs, just subtlety and long term goals, in order to save their necks.

Although hospitalisation prevented him answering the call to give evidence at the Nuremburg War Crimes trial in 1947, it did highlight the degree of damage one could sustain whilst working for the Germans at this Hell on Earth. Eventually Denis Avey received a cheque from the British government on account of 'compensation for Nazi persecution'. He was so deeply disgusted with the miserly amount of 204 pounds sterling that he sent the cheque straight back to the government.

Arthur Gifford-England

Sapper 1907124 Arthur H. Gifford-England, Royal Engineers, and later Auschwitz POW 221627, could claim the distinction of being the only inmate of E715 to cultivate a small garden outside his hut number 12. Sergeant Major Charlie Coward rewarded his enterprise by finding some tomato plants but, unfortunately, before they yielded the precious vegetable, they were destroyed by the digging of trenches because of an air raid.

One of Arthur's most amusing memories was of the German Propaganda Officer, who used to come in the camp telling the Brits the German twists on the latest War news. The POWs would heartily cheer every single item of news and this perceived mockery would so frustrate him that he jumped up and down in rage.

Another regular incident that brought a smile to the face of former Auschwitz POW 221627 were the not infrequent German hut searches while the lads were all absent at work. The Goons would find and confiscate a couple of radios made by the Signal Company from equipment stolen from I. G. Farben. Within two to three days the radios had been made up again, much to the chagrin of their hosts.

Ronald Albert Gaines

Jeff Gaines told Arthur about his father, Ronald Albert Gaines, Army number T/97824, yet another member of the RASC. Like so many of his colleagues from Monowitz, Ron would not talk about his experiences, preferring to withdraw into himself. As a driver with the RASC, his captivity was a long one, being caught up in the rearguard action at Dunkirk with the Jocks. Ron Gaines was involved in electrical work in the I. G. Farben complex. One of Jeff's most precious possessions is a 1933 Omega watch given to his late father by one of the many who went to the ovens.

The British would literally do anything they could think of, however bizarre, provided it cost the enemy time and caused them inconvenience. Ron Gaines provided a good example of this enterprising spirit: by urinating into moulds, resulting in explosions when molten metal was subsequently poured into them.

John (Jack) Stevens

Dr Phil Stevens, after consultation with his mother Joy, wrote of his late father, Grenadier Guardsman 2622083 John (Jack) Stevens, POW number 222251.

Jack, like Arthur Dodd, was taken prisoner in North Africa and eventually found himself captive in Monowitz Camp E714 and working for I. G. Farben. During Allied bombing, he was injured by receiving hot oil in both eyes and was taken to a local hospital. For the rest of his life Jack had white burn scars around his eyes.

Like many others, the sight of the hapless Jews clad only in thin pyjamas during intense cold weather made Jack sympathetic to their cause and he spoke to the internees and gave them food at great personal risk to himself.

As previously explained, there was more than one march to freedom and Jack was well behind Arthur Dodd, only arriving in Czechoslovakia in late May before eventually reaching home in late June 1945, resplendent in American uniform, having been released by General Patten's US tanks. He finished his Army career at the London headquarters for interviewing high ranking German personnel, commonly referred to as the 'cage'. Amongst the many that he guarded was one named Zacharias, who shot 30 POW British officers.

Soon after returning home their next door neighbour burnt the remains of the Sunday roast. Joy had to take Jack for a walk in a nearby forest because he could not differentiate between that particular smell and the one forever hanging over Monowitz from the crematoria at Auschwitz. Suddenly too many bad memories had come flooding back.

Jack Stevens was demobbed in the summer of 1946. He was diagnosed when first released as suffering from motor hysteria, caused in all probability by experiencing the horrors of Auschwitz. Motor hysteria is a condition where extreme anxiety is channelled in a physical reaction; in tremors, convulsions and a general shaking of the body. Whenever Jack ate, his stomach would swell up. Although often having nightmares, he spoke little of his experiences.

William Charles (Charlie) Hayward

Martin Haywood from County Durham made contact concerning his late father, William Charles Haywood, Army number T/10600672 and POW number 220148. Charlie's record of service showed he was a trooper and later a driver firstly in RECCE, then the RAC and finally in the RASC.

Charlie did enforced labour for I. G. Farben and also Heydebreck Buna IV Furstengrube and Janina mine. Charlie spoke little of life in Monowitz other than the 'extremely thin cabbage water', sabotage activities and the fact that he escaped three times.

Martin's only recollection of his father's comments about the Jewish prisoners, perhaps controversially, was their lack of comradeship, of sharing or helping each other when it came to any bits of food they were given by the British POWs.

Charlie Haywood went into the Army weighing nine and a half stone and came back at about six stone. After getting home he 'complained' about his mother nearly killing him with kindness by trying to feed him up so quickly. He had great difficulty keeping food down.

Bob Howse
Mr R.A. Howse told Arthur about his late father Bob Howse. An RASC driver and captured in North Africa like Arthur, Bob also worked at I. G. Farben where he befriended a male Jewish inmate. This hapless Jew made his English friend a ring which Bob wore for the rest of his life with pride and affection. As with all survivors of Monowitz, Bob Howse's quality of life was never the same post-war and he suffered deep depression, finally passing away in 1995.

John Best
Mary Best, John's widow, gave testament to the dramatic effect Auschwitz had on her beloved Geordie husband. He died eventually of emphysema caused by excessive

smoking due to the pressure of what he witnessed at that hellish destination, but not before he had experienced many harrowing nightmares. Mary would suddenly be violently woken by her husband shouting loudly and grabbing her hair with all his strength. The explanation was always the same when the situation had calmed down. John's nightmare involved him falling from a cliff edge and the grass he was grasping to save himself was his wife's hair.

On a lighter note, for her husband had never been a depressive, he would tell her of the occasion when a German guard broke some of his teeth with a rifle butt and he was in all probability the only POW who received new dentures made by the Red Cross!

Reference has been made previously to Arthur Dodd and like minded men continuing to fight the war from behind the wire in circumstances when it would have been easier not to do so. Archive searches of the United Nations War Crimes Commission have revealed Case number UK-G/B.219 and registered number 1479/UK/G/217. The documents indicate a breach of the laws and usages of war and in particular of Articles 2 and 46 of the Geneva Convention 1929 relative to the treatment of prisoners of war and have thrown up the name of Harry Ogden, No. 409353, the York and Lancaster Regiment, as being one of those committed to active resistance to the Nazis.

Harry Ogden was captured at Narvik in April 1940. After escaping two or three times and being recaptured each time, he eventually escaped from Camp E725 at Bismarckhutte in Upper

Silesia shortly before Christmas 1943. He spent about one year with Polish Partisans before being captured with some of them in Warsaw around September or October 1944 and taken to a Polish Concentration Camp at Auschwitz. He was the only British soldier in the Camp and vehemently stressed his British citizenship but, when captured, was armed and wearing Polish uniform. On arrival at Auschwitz he was interrogated three or four times but would only admit to being an Englishman in the British Army, to which his captors said that he should have more sense. He was taken with four Poles before the Camp Commandant, these five being assumed the ringleaders out of about fifty and sentenced to be flogged, each to receive 36 lashes. They were medically examined by the prison doctor before being taken out to the middle of the compound and put on a special wooden platform which had purposely been erected for floggings. They were put on the platform stripped to the waist and their wrists tied to a cross bar above their heads. Janck Novak was the first to be flogged, passing out before the regulation number of lashes, and he was followed by the British soldier. The flogging was a public one, all other prisoners being forced to attend, and a riding crop used to deliver the blows across the back. Hauptmann Georg Schwartz supervised the punishments and, after about eight lashes, Ogden fainted, eventually coming around in solitary confinement in a cell. The next day two guards came into the cell and questioned him as to where he had joined the Resistance Movement and from whom had he received his arms. He refused to tell them anything and one of the guards knocked him down with his fist before both of them kicked him in the face and on the shoulders and body. The perpetrators of the beatings wore slacks and shoes and had no marks of rank or unit on their uniforms. The blows knocked out two of Ogden's teeth and cut the bridge of his nose.

On the following day he was again taken out and flogged in similar fashion and this was repeated again on the fifth day after the first flogging. Ogden did not know how many blows he received at the second and third floggings because he fainted each time. Remaining in solitary confinement for three weeks, he was given only bread and water, one piece of bread at breakfast and two at tea. He was not examined by the medical officer after any of the floggings nor before the second and third punishments. Ogden remained in the concentration camp at Auschwitz for about five or six weeks before being taken with the other four Poles to Stalag 8B at Teschen in Czechoslovakia. In January 1945 the five were sent to detention prison at Graudenz and tried by military court for manslaughter. Private Ogden was awarded 14 years imprisonment and the five brave men all sent back to Graudenz to await disposal but were rescued by the Russians three days after they returned.

Harry Ogden from Halifax in Yorkshire was yet another Brit, so similar to Arthur Dodd, to never stop fighting the war, a fact of which everyone from our small island can be truly proud.

There were two instances of war crimes involving the British in Auschwitz and these were duly turned over to the War Crimes Investigation Unit on the 6 January 1947. The National Archives reference is WO309/1063 and the accused, Unteroffizier Benno Franz, is common to both acts and charges. Lance-Corporal Reynolds was shot and killed whilst Private Campbell was seriously wounded by bayoneting in the back when carrying a Dixie of soup for a frail Polish girl unable to cope with the weight.

The killing of Lance-Corporal Reynolds took place in the I. G. Farben works at Auschwitz where the work party was employed on constructional work. He was killed in cold blood by Franz because he refused to work on steel girders, 70 feet up, in winter conditions and without proper safety equipment. Dr Lothar Kurt Gotthold Heinrich was employed at the I. G. Farben factory and was responsible, among other things, for the provision of safety belts for men employed on overhead constructional work.

In 1947 German POW, Lothar Kurt Gotthold Heinrich, was detained at Internment Camp No. 78, Zuffenhausen. The following is the description of Dr Heinrich:

Civilian occupation – Chemist employed by I. G. Farben; aged about fifty; dark hair, going grey and worn closely cropped; wears glasses; pale complexion; speaks English; member of the Nazi party; a typical research chemist. The POW claimed to be a constructional engineer and architect, had no knowledge of chemistry and was never employed by I. G. Farbenindustrie. Since the physical description and the three Christian names of the two Dr Heinrichs were identical, it was recommended that Dr Heinrich would be of assistance in tracing the accused, Benno Franz. It is not known whether Unteroffizier Benno Franz was ever found and brought to justice.

PART THREE: SNAPSHOTS FROM AFFIDAVITS GIVEN UNDER OATH AT NUREMBERG

In general the British POWs made a positive impression on I. G. Farben plant managers although security, not surprisingly, kept them under a watchful eye. In November 1944 the British Red Cross Society made a marked understatement about the huge undertaking, saying that E715 performed 'constructional work for a local firm'. In post war statements the veterans devoted little attention to their own labour. Typical was Charles Hill's somewhat subdued statement at Nuremberg: 'I worked for the I. G. Farben factory, first on the cable gang and later on general labour.'

If the labour the British had been forced to perform did not prompt much post war reflection, the treatment of concentration camp inmates was permanently burnt into their memories. A shocking sight greeted all the British POWs on their very first day at the factory. Wearing thin blue and gray striped uniforms that afforded little or no protection against the harsh elements in that part of Silesia, emaciated Monowitz inmates, predominately Jewish, toiled under kapos and meisters who beat them to extract as much work as possible before their deaths. The British saw fallen inmates, their eyes lifeless, strewn about the plant. On one day alone they counted no fewer than thirty dead and dying. These pathetic images of excessively inhuman treatment from one human being to another stayed with the lads returning to Britain and indeed, in numerous cases had an even greater disturbance on their minds in later years. The Jews' physical debilitation made every step a mountain to climb and labour sheer torture, something exacerbated by Farben management's insatiable demand for performance. 'Once the inmates were assigned they became the slave of each respective Meister,' said Leonard Dales, a member of the POW delegation at the Nuremburg War Crimes trial and one who received a detailed description of the Birkenau killing center from a Dutch Jew, who asked Leonard to 'tell the rest of the world what had happened'. Because of their striped garb some of the Brits called them 'stripees' whilst others preferred the chilling expression 'working corpses'. Cliff Shepherd recalled yet another ironically sarcastic reference. 'The Jews were known as the "Healthy Life Boys", because in the Red Cross parcels from Sterling in Scotland there were tins of biscuits with striped packaging called ""Healthy Life Biscuits".' Horace Charters made the following observation with respect to the low levels of strength to which the 'stripees' had sunk, 'so weak were they that a dozen of them would struggle to pick up a pipe that three to four of our boys could pick up without too much trouble.' When it came to laying cables Charles Hill emphasized the totally unfair lot of the Jew: 'While we were placed one man to each foot of cable, the inmates were located one man to the yard.' Frederick Wellard summarised the lot of the Jew in the racial hierarchy at I. G. Farben: 'all treatment of Jews was mistreatment.'

Eric Doyle, another who represented the POWs at Nuremburg, had the intensely unsettling experience of seeing someone he recognized from peacetime in striped uniform. 'He was a lightweight fighter whom I had seen fight in 1938. In 1943 I saw him as an inmate in Auschwitz. He was on the same working party as myself. I never saw a bigger wreck of any kind. I should say he had both arms broken, his shoulders were bowed like an old man, and he looked to be about fifty years old. I would not have recognized him if I had not known it was he. He disappeared and I don't know what happened to him. There were quite a lot of cases of disappearance like that.'

All 'stripees' were familiar with the slogan 'not fit to work, not fit to live'. When Cliff Shepherd first saw concentration camp inmates after his transfer to E715 in January 1944, he naturally assumed they were 'convicts'. A meister disabused him: 'When I first arrived I asked one of the Germans who the men were in these striped uniforms. He said they were Jews, the 'Parasites' as he called them... I said, 'What have they done wrong?' He says, "They're Jews." I said, "Why are they working in forced labour?" He said, "Because they're rotten...They're the dregs of the earth...They've bled Germany dry... They've got to be gassed when they can't work any more." I said, "How do they gas them?" He said, "They put them in a chamber, like a tank, and seal it." It distressed me a lot. It still does.'

The casual brutality witnessed at the plant was just the beginning. Once relocated to Lager VI (E715), the British heard shootings and screams from Monowitz at night. They also saw hanging victims dangling beside the camp gate. In G. J. Duffree's words, 'From our compound we could see the hanging rail, where they often strung up their victims and left them...' So pervasive was the Nazi racial barbarism that it assaulted practically every sense. The British saw the beatings; they heard the meisters say the Jews were just getting what they deserved; they tasted the Buna soup, the inmates' midday ration; and they experienced the acrid smoke that regularly drifted over I. G. Farben from Birkenau. There was no escaping that pungent odour. So desperate were the 'stripees' for food that a charitable act sometimes sparked a melee, as G. J. Duffree discovered: 'We fed them as much as we could spare, but I've seen the poor bastards fight to the death for a potato.'

For a POW, a cigarette could be either a consumable item or a currency in the Stalag economy, because such luxuries were more common in the POW camp; but for a concentration camp inmate it equated to a day's rations on the plant's black market. 'Stripees' bartered Red Cross cigarettes for bread or other food as part of what they called their 'organising' activities. With an anti-Semitic undertone W. N. Davis observed: 'The most amazing part of the trading in the factory was the fact that although the Jewish 'Stripees' were the worst off in the place, they were the ones who did nearly all of the deals.'

Reginald Hartland worked with Norbert Wollheim, a Jewish inmate in Monowitz from March 1943, who had volunteered to work on the building site as a welder in order to contact the British POWs. Working together in Workshop 797, the two became very close. Wollheim had learnt English in school and, just before the outbreak of war, had assisted the emigration of German-Jewish children to Great Britain. On hearing about E715, he used connections inside Monowitz to join a kommando that worked alongside POWs. Wollheim passed on to Hartland all the information he knew about the Nazi treatment of the Jews, together with war news from Nazi papers discarded at the building site, while Hartland reciprocated in kind with news from the BBC, obtained from a secret radio in E715. The German Jew told his British friend time and again his same thoughts, 'You'll probably be able to survive because you're under the protection of the Red Cross.' So close did the two become that Hartland informed Wollheim's family in the United States as to his whereabouts. Their friendship survived the war, having reunions at the I. G. Farben trial at Nuremburg in 1947 and a 1962 BBC 'This is Your Life' episode that honoured Charles Coward, the E715 Camp Leader.

Since there were seventeen times as many Monowitz inmates as British POWs by late 1944, the British soldiers (or kriegies to which they were sometimes referred) could help precious few of the hapless Jews. Ronald Redman echoed the frustration of many by stating, 'Gradually as one got accustomed to them in their prolific numbers, one hardened as it was not possible to provide all of them with a cigarette, a piece of clothing, food, or unwanted soup. Despite this they seemed to regard us as having unlimited means, knowledge of the war, even to sheep-like following during an air-raid as we knew where the bombs were going to fall!'

Those who had nothing naturally looked upon the British as a privileged group. Primo Levi described a kriegie he encountered in a plant lavatory: the captive soldier wore a smart uniform, displayed a military bearing, and appeared to be the picture of health. The POW, in his estimation, inhabited another world. Levi went on to observe that some concentration camp inmates 'cultivated' the POWs, raising panhandling to high art form. Young Henri, one of the most memorable persons in his testimony, employed guile and 'pity' to obtain food and other valuables from many on the job site, especially POWs. Thanks to 'wealthy' benefactors, Henri was able to eat well by Monowitz standards. He 'was once seen in the act of eating a real hard boiled egg,' a prize that might well have taken a roundabout course from British barter with Polish workers.

'Manna' was how Norbert Wollheim described British generosity and encouragement, adding that: 'England can be very, very proud of these men, who really proved that even in Auschwitz humanity could prevail... The British extended the hand of solidarity of man to Monowitz inmates.'

British help in time of need sometimes had unfortunate, even tragic, consequences. One POW who accidentally incurred SS wrath and brought disaster on an inmate was Frank Harris. 'I myself have two scars on my face, chin and left eyebrow, for giving a young Jewish inmate, thirteen years of age, a hand to get to his feet after falling down through weakness. The SS guard shot him and rifle-butted me in the face.'

Dr Ian Osborne Spencer RAMC was the medical man who nursed Arthur Dodd miraculously and painstakingly through pneumonia and who, on his first day in Lager VIII, was taken to one side by an I. G. Farben official; he was told in clear and no uncertain terms that in order to meet necessary production efficiency, he had to keep the sick list, those permitted to abstain from work, to a maximum of 3 per cent. The sick list was in effect often between 10 and 15 per cent and, in order to meet necessary production efficiency, a Doctor Bonk, who was an employee of I. G. Farben, acting in the capacity of an assistant to Dr Poeschel, would re-examine the unfit in an examination lasting only 30 seconds per man. The 3 per cent target would then be met by German guards with fixed bayonettes marching the designated POWs off to the I. G. Farben factory. POW Dennis Greenham confirmed the statement by Dr Spencer in his own affidavit, 'I was one of a group of British lads that were forced to work at the point of a gun, after being declared unfit by our own doctor. I had fever and chills at the time.'

Robert Robertson was a lieutenant in the RAMC and was captured at St Valery in Normandy, the very same site as Doddie's first volunteering mission, on 12 June 1940. The Scot worked with Dr Spencer at Auschwitz from September 1943 to April 1944 and confirmed the latter's affivdavit statement regarding the maximum 3 per cent sick list and the German 30-second medical examinations.

Frederick Wooley in his statement dismissed any doubts that some people were unaware of what was going on at Auschwitz. 'When the big shot Farben officials came on inspection tours together with military personnel, there was no attempt made to hide the unpalatable state of the inmates or to conceal the abominable working conditions. To be ignorant of what was going on was never even a remote possibility to anyone, Jew and Gentile alike. Kapos, Meisters and SS, in order to extract more effort from the inmate slaves, used to threaten them verbally with a visit to the gas chambers.'

Leonard Dales from the Lincolnshire Regiment was a labourer at I. G. Farben to a German pipe engineer. In this capacity he had work details to perform in all parts of the factory, providing excellent opportunities to gain an overview of working conditions and the incredible levels of depravity of the Jews. He recalled one incident when one of his colleagues tossed a cigarette to a Jew who was loading some pipes. The unfortunate wretch scrambled down, intent on grabbing the precious commodity and, in doing so, badly lacerated his leg. The inmate didn't seem so much hurt as scared as he muttered, 'I guess this is the end, it means the gas chamber for me.' He was never seen again at the workplace.

One Dutch Jew who had worked in very close proximity to the gas chambers told Dales of the sham of the Nazis offering the doomed Jews soap and a towel in order to maintain the pretence of the showering facility. Many times when the inmates realized what was happening, terrible scenes of panic would take place, but they were nevertheless forced into the gas chambers at pistol point by the sadistic SS. This Jew ended his message most poignantly by telling Dales that he didn't think he would ever get out alive but he knew that some of the British POWs would and he wanted these survivors to tell the world what had happened at Auschwitz.

British POWs received better treatment than Poles, Russians and other Eastern European nations who, in turn, were far better off than the greatly oppressed Jews. The Nazis were not slow in demoting prisoners from their fair treatment position for any misdemeanor and Kenneth Lovell, Corporal in the Durham Light Infantry, was an example of this. Lovell escaped from Stalag 383 in Bavaria, was caught and sentenced to death at Regensburg for escaping and having a weapon and illegal documents in his possession. A change of heart from the German authorities saw him transferred to Auschwitz, where his head was shorn and he received a striped inmate suit with a black triangle and the letters XKGF, which designated him a former POW. He was not considered a POW anymore and was treated like any other concentration camp inmate. Lovell worked at Auschwitz for 24 days with Poles, Yugoslavs and Serbs, all of whom were under sentence of death. The group were struck by SS guards and German civilians with rifle butts, wooden sticks and even iron bars. The Durham man was later transferred to Dachau from where he escaped and survived until liberated by the Americans.

Another example of German retribution was witnessed by British POW Dennis Greenham, who stated that forced labourers may have been given some liberties but they had no choice when it came down to work. Greenham added, 'I knew one fellow, a Polish non-Jew, who stayed away from work for five days. As punishment he was converted from a "free" worker to a concentration camp inmate for a six month sentence. In effect he was then a virtual Jewish inmate and unlikely to survive.'

Israel Majzlik was a Polish Jew with slightly better food privileges because he was a foreman. On the 28 February 1944 he was found in building 850 at I. G. Farben sitting and smoking near the fire together with a detainee and an Englishman. He was given 15 cane strokes and permanent underground work from then on.

Lancastrian John Pascoe noted that, with the exception of the Jews, the worst treated race at Auschwitz was the Russians and in particular the girls who worked close to Pascoe's site. They refilled cement bags and carried them to another part of the building to be restacked. All they wore were cotton frocks and, even in the most bitter of winter's blasts, they had no other clothing. They used to use the torn cement sacks, which were just stiff paper, to wrap around their bodies to keep warm. During the time Pascoe was at that site he could see these girls, although quite strong initially, becoming weaker and thinner all the time.

Liverpool born Horace Reginald Charters was Company Sergeant Major for the 8th Battalion Worcestershire Regiment and was captured at Dunkirk. At Auschwitz he held an administrative position, having been placed in charge of the British POWs as a Vortrauensmann, a position of authority. In this capacity, his duties included looking after the complaints of the men concerning their working conditions, clothing and food. 'There were a great number of complaints and most of them were justified. The food was inadequate and if it were not for the fact that they received Red Cross packages, it would have been very difficult for our boys to get along, especially if they were to keep on working. They didn't supply us with clothing and only in a very few cases would they give us boots even when the work involved often standing in mud and water up to their waists carrying pipes and laying pipelines.'

Walther Duerrfeld joined I. G. Farbenindustrie (usually referred to as I. G. Farben) in 1927 as a machine construction engineer and by 1932 had become chief of the workshops for the entire high pressure plant. About March 1941 Duerrfeld was made Technical Manager of the construction of the Auschwitz Plant and in spring 1944 was appointed Director. The new Auschwitz facility was planned to produce thirty thousand tons of Buna per annum and decisive for the choice of the area was the existence of natural resources, coal and lime in the vicinity, water from the Vistula and ample workers from Silesia and beyond. In 1941 Duerrfeld estimated that a total of between thirteen and sixteen thousand workers would be needed for Auschwitz. At a meeting in Berlin between Duerrfeld, two more senior colleagues, Heinrich Buetefisch and Oberingenieur Faust and SS-Obergruppenfuehrer Wolf discussed the employment of concentration camp inmates. It was agreed that the supervision of these inmates was to be carried out by the SS, and that no connection should exist between these inmates and the other workers. A daily price of RM 3 (3 Reich Marks) for each unskilled and RM 4 for each skilled concentration camp inmate was fixed. This price was accepted by I. G. Farben and the aggregate of all the monies was paid monthly to the SS in Berlin. This economic package suited the Third Reich admirably; the SS had a seemingly non-ending supply of free Jewish labour, were paid well by I. G. Farben and simultaneously achieved the ultimate eradication of a despised race. The building commissions for I. G. Auschwitz were allocated by Santo, the leading construction engineer, to nearly one hundred and fifty construction companies which also employed concentration camp inmates.

Farben also employed foreign workers including local Poles, Russians, Frenchmen, Belgians, Italians and Croats amongst others. These men lived in enclosed camps within the 25-square-mile Auschwitz complex. A 15 per cent deduction was taken from the Polish wages and sent to Berlin but from the Russian wages the SS in Berlin benefited by an incredible 30 per cent or even 40 per cent at times. From 1943, British POWs were also employed by I. G. Auschwitz and they were housed in three separate camps numbered VIII, IV and VI, the latter being the closest to the Farben factory, some 300 yards from its main gate and designated E715. Monowitz camps were surrounded by electrically barbed wire and each had four or six watch towers, each one occupied by one SS sentry. Duerrfeld claimed he was interested in being informed about any deaths of workers at Monowitz but added that he was never informed of any. 'Until nearly the end of 1942, the SS was exclusively responsible for feeding the concentration camp inmates of Monowitz. From then on I. G. Auschwitz took over the purchase of the food according to the ration coupons provided by the SS, and the supervision of the food preparation at the Camp Kitchen Monowitz. I myself saw by means of the menus, that the daily number of calories of the concentration camp inmates amounted to at least 2800. I have never doubted that they got them, but I do not know it. I have often watched the distribution of the plant produced soup (*werkssuppe*) to the concentration camp inmates at the I. G. Plant.' Duerrfeld later stated that he visited this camp between five and ten times during its total existence. He also stated that he met with Hoess, Commandant of Auschwitz, on between ten and fifteen occasions, advising on housing of Jews in closer proximity to their work areas in order to improve their overall performance, short marches meaning less risk of Spotted Fever (Typhus) and diminished psychic oppression.

Christian Schneider, senior to Duerrfeld, was a member of the Central Committee and Commissioner thereof for all social problems of the entire I. G. Farbenindustrie from 1938-1945. He was one of those who took the decision to build the fourth Buna Plant at Auschwitz rather than enlarge any or all of the existing three Buna factories, for decentralizing the production ensured that any one plant did not carry a disproportionately high production aliquot. The motive for this decision was fear of enemy air raids. Although the plant was to be built on Polish territory, the Central Committee did not raise any objection to the compulsory evacuation of the Polish population, nor to the collaboration with the

SS. After 1941 Schneider recollected that it was not unusual for I. G. to employ concentration camp inmates, as was also the case with numerous other German companies on site. Schneider stated that he was aware that those people of varying social status were held in concentration camps for political and racial reasons. The money for setting up the Monowitz concentration camp went through Schneider via an ordinary credit procedure and the value of the credits together with the general limited quality of the huts meant the latter were destined for camp prisoners. Regarding the state of the inmates, Schneider observed that some were worn out and overworked people, while others still looked reasonable. He did state that he had heard of camp prisoners being beaten on the I. G. building site, adding that although in work mode prisoners were under I. G. supervision, in disciplinary respects, they were at the dubious mercy of the SS.

Schneider granted money for a brothel at Monwitz, this being intended for Polish workers. Russians, mainly Ukrainians, were employed at I. G. Farben but, because of the hatred existing between German and Russian, the latter were never granted any leave at all. Any Czech or French labour sent under compulsory work orders was made on the basis of agreements concluded between the two countries, thus corresponding to compulsory conscription. Schneider added that no work contracts in the usual meaning of the word were concluded with these workers. Foreign workers at I. G. Auschwitz were segregated according to nationality but Jews were accommodated in a special camp.

Schneider could not recall if the question was ever discussed regarding whether it was not permissible under the Geneva or the Hague Conventions respectively to employ Prisoners of War in armament undertakings. He had heard, however, from Walther Duerrfeld and other engineers that they personally did smell the odour emanating from the crematoria in Birkenau. All these gentlemen described the experience as disgustingly nauseating.

PART FOUR:
RESPONSES TO
ARTHUR'S STORY

The first edition of *Spectator in Hell* and the evidence of Arthur's great faith were well received by the public. In addition, Arthur's story has contributed to a better understanding of the unspeakable horrors that fathers and husbands returning from the war were unable to share with their families. Younger generations have been appreciative of the incredible story made available to them and their good fortune in being born in more settled times. Excerpts from some of the letters received are reproduced below.

Mrs Ann Graham wrote from Newcastle on Tyne regarding her late father, William (Bill) Lemin, who found himself in the same Camp VI (E715) as Arthur Dodd and indeed, the two were enthusiastic members of Taffy's choir.

Dad told the family about the black bread and potato soup. He never liked potatoes for the rest of his life, dying in 1970 aged fifty-one. He told us quite a bit about his life as a POW, but he never, ever mentioned any of the atrocities he must have seen and heard. I don't know whether he found talking about them too difficult to cope with. He was basically a cheerful, happy, loving man; he did suffer from depression at times and I often wonder if this was the reason. A chap who loved singing, he performed in some of the camp concerts.

Another name on the Auschwitz concert programme, immediately below that of Bill Lemin, was that of the late Walter C. Martin, whose story is told by his son-in-law, Bernard Scarborough from Surrey.

Walter had already been a member of a Concert Party whilst confined in two camps in Italy. He well knew the immense responsibility shouldered by these entertainers in helping maintain a reasonable level of morale in the most horrendous of circumstances. And he soon realised that Auschwitz was no ordinary concentration camp; its sights and sounds eating away at men's minds and pushing them towards insanity.

In the Auschwitz Concert Party, a prominent role was played by the 'The Three T's', a music group consisting of two Townies and a Taff. In a talent show at the camp, this trio had excelled sufficiently to take first prize, with Walter Martin on the harmonica and the Taff from the Welsh Guards playing the guitar. One of the judges of the contest was Camp Leader Charlie Coward who always strove to optimise the entertainment of his men. In November 1944, with the invasion of Europe going so well for the Allies, Walter wrote a little number entitled 'Six Weeks To Go'. Although a little optimistic as events were to prove, this cheerful rendition went down well in the camp, with even the band playing it.

Gillian Hatch from Athens in Greece wrote in reference to her father.

When I came across your book *Spectator in Hell* it was as if it had been sitting there waiting for me, so that a few more pieces of the jigsaw could be added, something I have been longing for ever since I learnt that my father was one of the British POWs held at Auschwitz.

I would probably never have discovered this horrific chapter of his past had it not been for a letter sent to my father six years ago by an American who was researching into the very same subject. He had apparently obtained my father's name from the Nottingham branch of the National Ex-POW Association. In 1994 only 32 of these survivors remained. The person in question sent my father a detailed questionnaire to answer, which was covered by most of Arthur Dodd's account.

In my father's case his war experiences seemed to have weakened rather than strengthened his character. He and my mother were in their forties when they began a family and I always had the feeling, even as a young child, that I and my sister were too much for our father. In fact, the whole responsibility was just too much for him and he would opt out in his own way, leaving our mother to take charge. These long silences persist to this day and, although he is definitely more content in retirement than he ever was before, there are still periods of 'absence' when it is difficult to reach him.

As children we knew that our father had served in the Army during World War Two and that he was a POW in

Poland. Concentration camps, least of all Auschwitz, were never alluded to, not even when I chose to go and work on a Kibbutz in Israel. It was my obsession with learning about the Holocaust, and the considerable amount of literature I had already read, that added to the shock of discovering that my own father had been held there. It was a macabre coincidence or link between my father's past and my own present, one which I am still puzzling over. Your book was a particularly valuable find for me as I've been able to piece together some of my father's experiences through Mr Dodd's own recollections. Since I cannot bring myself to raise the subject with my father, this document has an even greater significance.

I clearly remember the first comment I made to my father after reading the American researcher's letter: 'I didn't know there were British POWs held at Auschwitz.' It is still a shock and my father has always saved half of the meat from one meal for the next day. We used to laugh at him when we were children, but he would always insist that he wasn't hungry.

Canon John Griffith from Cheshire wrote a brief note to Arthur.

I find your book very interesting and moving. I salute you! I admire you and thank you for expressing your strong faith to so many via your life's story. You are of great encouragement, I am proud of you.

Jim Costen from Gravesend, another British POW survivor from Auschwitz, confirms Arthur's story.

I was in the same factory as him in Auschwitz. I was captured in the desert at the same place, was also in Italy and was on that 700-mile march. I escaped in Czechoslovakia. What he said was all true, I am the same age as him and would like to compare our stories.

Arthur had the good fortune to meet up with Bill Meredith, another E715 survivor, and the son of Reg Owen, extreme right on the back row of the included photograph of the Camp's England football team. Bill Meredith assured the author immediately that he remembered Arthur in E715 with his tell tale characteristic limp, before continuing to recall the hazardous day he experienced within the first week of arriving in Monowitz. He witnessed a German guard being particularly brutal with a gaunt and hapless Jew, clearly so weak that his maker would soon be calling him. The lad from Liverpool watched for a seemingly endless few minutes before his temper boiled over and he floored the Nazi with a crisp punch clean on the jaw. Sensing the ensuing inevitable trouble, all the Brits immediately regrouped around the scouser. When the German came around a full inspection of inmates was ordered but, with the group only being there days and everyone having had their heads shaved, the victim was unable to identify his assailant, much to the relief of one lucky son of Liverpool.

Reg Owen's son of the same name chatted away to Arthur, each relating a flood of memories. Reg Owen Senior, no mean accordion player, found a large Hohner accordion on the march whilst passing through a bombed-out hotel. His playing contributed greatly to sing-songs which, in the most difficult of circumstances, helped flagging morale no end. Later on, however, the then critically starving POWs were more than grateful to exchange their joyful instrument for some of life's essentials, especially food.

27-year-old Melaina Cartwright from Leeds revealed her increased interest in World War Two since reading Arthur's account.

> I have just finished reading your book *Spectator in Hell*, and would like to say what a brilliant book it is. I have read a lot of books on Auschwitz and other camps but I don't think any of them touched me as much as Mr Dodd's ordeal. When you read the book it is as if you're there living it with Mr Dodd. I could never imagine what life would be like in a camp such as Auschwitz. I don't think I would want to. At school we were not allowed to read or learn anything about Hitler's Final Solution. It is wrong not to learn, because to me, it is a big part of history. It is a big part that I don't think will ever be erased, and it shouldn't. Your book is the first I have read about British POWs being in the Death Camps. I think people were so ignorant at the end of the war when Mr Dodd came home that they just didn't want to believe what these camps were like.
>
> I would like to say thank you to him for telling his story. I know some people would rather forget about certain things from the war, but to me, I don't think that is right. My generation needs the likes of Mr Dodd to tell us.

SPECTATOR IN HELL

Ellen Trump wrote to Arthur from Libramont-Chevigny in Belgium.

> I am a student living in Belgium with my family, and I have just read the book Colin Rushton wrote about your extraordinary story during World War Two, *Spectator in Hell*. It really touched me.
>
> I am a Christian too, and the testimony of your faith in God during such awful times really encouraged me.
>
> So then, those who suffer because it is God's will for them, should by their good actions trust themselves completely to their Creator, who always keeps his promise.
>
> 1 Peter 4:19
>
> Looking forward to meeting you in Heaven.

Mrs Beryl Brew put pen to paper from Salisbury in Wiltshire.

> Both my husband and I read your book, *Spectator in Hell*, with interest as it answered a lot of questions that my husband's family always wanted to know.
>
> My husband's brother, Allen Brew RN from the Isle of Man, was also a prisoner in Auschwitz, and was also one of the few who survived the march. When he returned home to the Island he would not talk of his experiences to anyone. At night he also had terrible nightmares which stayed with him until he died in 1965 of cancer.
>
> In 1997 my husband and I went on a trip to Poland where we visited the camp for Jews. It was only by talking to the guide that we discovered there were three camps,

and that number three was where the POWs were held. We were unable to go to this camp so therefore could find out nothing more.

After reading your book we can now understand the suffering that he went through, and his reasons for not talking about it.

So thank you for writing it, it has helped one family at least to understand what their loved one went through.

Avril Separzadeh communicated with Arthur from California.

I don't know if you remember me or not – I am Taffy Williams' daughter, Avril. My name is now Avril Separzadeh (a Jewish name).

I was privileged to read your book that Dad had mailed to me. I felt your pain and sadness to have witnessed such cruelty from one human being to another. War is a terrible thing and books like yours will show the world of such horrors and inhumane brutality. I am glad you found it in your heart to write it with Colin Rushton's help. I am sure and hope that you felt a burden lifted from your heart.

Survivors of concentration camps are constantly literally relieved to share their stories. All of them feel a huge weight lifted from them, like a cleansing from pain. I hope you feel that relief.

Having married into the Jewish faith, my life now revolves around Judaism and we are proud to raise our children as good, caring and wonderful people. This may never have been made possible if it had not been for generous people like yourself who fought in the war to liberate all people.

Nicholas Rolls from Farnborough corresponded with Arthur regarding his father.

My father, Ivor Herbert Rolls, was a prisoner of war in Stallag IVB at Auschwitz for twenty months. My father, like yourself, is not from Jewish descent and was born in England. He grew up in Salisbury, Wiltshire and was an electrician and mechanic before the war. At the start of the war he joined the Royal Signals as a signalman (Army number, 2587701) and after his training went out to Africa where he served for about six months before he was captured in Tobruk, Libya by the German Army. After being imprisoned in Italy he eventually ended up in Auschwitz.

My father took great interest in your book and found it very emotional. He is a quiet, dignified man who I have never seen cry until he took up your book. This is partly why I have written to you so that, through me, we can all share these enlightening stories of World War Two and perhaps get to know each other.

Another person feeling strongly about Arthur Dodd's account was Marieanne Vale writing from Coleford in Gloucestershire about her father, Richard (Dick) Whiffin.

I read your book when it was first published, just after the death of my Dad. It gave me a much better insight into the experiences he suffered during the war. Like Arthur he was captured in the desert and imprisoned in Italy, from where he landed up in Auschwitz. He never referred to his experiences except the shooting of the Brit who refused to climb frozen telegraph poles without proper safety equipment. All his life he never forgot the face of the German who shot this principled British POW, for he carried the newspaper cutting of the incident all his life. I remember Dad was friendly with a Polish man while there and he also carried his picture always.

My Dad was really proud of the fact that the men had sabotaged the work they were forced to do for I. G. Farben. With a glint in his eye he also mentioned that the Camp Commandant had a dog that mysteriously disappeared after wandering into the camp as though that too was part and parcel of the sabotage program! Richard Whiffin was a signaler originally from Hebburn on Tyne but living during the war in Kent.

Thank you for writing about Arthur's experiences in the camp, it must have been hard for him to relate the daily horrors to which they were exposed. At least people now believe that British soldiers were there. I am really proud of my Dad and understand why, every now and then, he would go off for a drink, it was his therapy and none of us in the family begrudged him that. We all loved him deeply and will never forget him.

Thank you for letting me tell you about Dad.

Another grateful letter, dated 22 July 1999, was addressed to the author from Jean Boesch from Ontario in Canada.

I have just finished reading your book *Spectator in Hell*. It was given to my Dad to read by his brother Alfred C. Stow, who remembered Mr Dodd from the prison camp. Uncle Alf is also one of that small number of Auschwitz survivors who is still alive. He now lives with his wife in Canada and will be seventy-nine years of age in November 1999. He has never spoken at great lengths about his experiences in the prison camps, but from the little he has told us we understand that he was held captive six months by the Italians, and three years by the Germans. On a couple of the pages in the book he has written, 'I also slept here', and 'both these incidents happened to me'.

Uncle Alf worked with Ronald Redman under a supervisor who took a laissez-faire approach, allowing his charges the run of the plant, which afforded them great opportunities for mischief. Alf was one of the fortunate few who was allowed to work in the electrical shop and learn new skills regarding workshop practice and the use of tools and metals, experience that served him well in later life. While in the main the German meisters approved of the extermination campaign against the Jews, Uncle Alf encountered a few who, while anti-Semitic, professed to deplore the Nazi tactics. In fact, one with whom Uncle Alf was particularly close expressed utter contempt for the Nazis. Many others clearly identified with the regime and employed stock rationalisations to justify racial barbarism when addressing the enquiring British.

Thank you for bringing to public awareness the atrocities of that horrible war. Our modern generation needs to know about such horrors to be able to avoid them in the future. A big thank you to Mr Arthur Dodd for allowing us to live through his experiences with him, and for sharing his faith with us. May our Lord continue to bless him and heal him of everything he suffered.

In his extremely eventful wartime service, the occasion that most fills Arthur with sadness and visibly moves him emotionally was the tragic loss of life of those brave POWs who, by 1944, had endured so much. The impact of one particular August day was brought vividly back to him via a letter from Mrs J. Thomas from north Wales. Her uncle, 1888095 Sapper Frederick Hughes of the Royal Engineers, was one of those killed on what should have been such a happy day, celebrating the D-Day landings and the push into Europe. Arthur realised that Fred Hughes must have been toward the opposite end of the shelter in which they were hiding from an air-raid; the end that took the worst of the blast. A day of triumph had turned to one of tragedy and Arthur still had that emptiness and anger in the pit of his stomach after hearing about this victim from North Wales.

The ignorance regarding the British at Auschwitz was born out of, in the main, skeletal survivors withdrawing into themselves after their eyes had witnessed indescribable atrocities, extreme even for a theatre of war. Others, like Arthur Dodd, tried to tell people about Auschwitz but nobody wanted to know, least of all the British military. This was emphasised in Mrs Thomas's letter. Her nephew was around twelve years of age in 1992/3 when his class were discussing World War Two. The lad related what had been common knowledge in their family for many years, the fact that his great uncle Fred had been killed in Auschwitz by an Allied bomb. He was chastised by the teacher for telling lies, which caused him some distress.

George Alexander Saunders was the subject of a letter written by his niece, Mrs. Yvonne Winson, from Cambridgeshire. Sandy, as he was generally known, was Gunner 889720 of the Royal Artillery, a regular soldier before the war, enlisting on the 17 March 1939. He was captured on June 6 1942 in Bir Harmet in the 'cauldron' at Knightsbridge, after earlier surviving the first siege of Tobruk, before eventually becoming an unwilling inmate of Auschwitz. The legacies this satanic destination bequeathed to Sandy included suffering the consequences of frostbite to his hands and feet for the rest of his life. In addition were the agonies of deformity of his feet due to wearing incorrectly sized boots. The boots were issued by the Germans from a list order, when your name came up you received the next available pair of boots, whatever the size, without a sign of dissension… unless you wanted a rifle butt across your face or in your kidneys.

On arrival at Auschwitz Sandy, who had been a cinema

projectionist in London, claimed he was an engineer, possibly as a means to access a position offering sabotage possibilities. Together with his 'mucker', Frankie Merrill, Sandy made an escape attempt during Allied air raids in late 1944 when spotting an unattended fire engine not one hundred yards from the camp gates. The two escape-minded Brits soon found out why the vehicle was unattended, it was completely devoid of fuel! They crept back into camp somewhat disenchanted but nevertheless better there than being shot by unpredictable Russian soldiers.

Having worked under an older German civilian in the factory, Sandy had learnt a good measure of the German language. This German civilian was quite kind to the British lads but only when the guards were not around. During the latter part of 1944 this older civilian was allowed a pass to go home but told he would be shot if he did not return. When he did get back he was very quiet and Sandy asked him why. Apparently his home had been demolished by Allied bombing and his wife and daughter were missing presumed dead. Although Sandy was in a German POW camp and had relations who were in the London blitz, this compassionate Brit felt sorry for this older man who was as much a victim of Hitler's regime as any of the enemies of the Third Reich.

As a regular soldier, when he had partially recovered from his wartime exploits he was sent on various 'evaluations', one of which was in Newcastle, to see if he was of sane mind. George Saunders, POW 221777, having come home with malnutrition, pleurisy, pneumonia and frostbite after serving his country, was discharged from the army for 'ceasing to fulfill army physical requirements'. A small pension was awarded to Sandy on discharge but two years later a review conducted by 'Colonel Blimp' type characters in Whitehall cancelled that pension because he was able to work. Despite Sandy appealing that he had to work to support his wife and children, his protest was turned down.

In October 1997 Yvonne Winson persuaded Sandy to re-apply for a war pension as his health was deteriorating. The pension was eventually granted in July 1998 but sadly Sandy did not have the benefit of his pension for long, passing away on 12 April 2000. Yvonne finishes her letter 'I will always remember a very special man'.

PART FIVE:
THE BRITISH
GOVERNMENT'S
TREATMENT OF
SURVIVORS

The most poignant and distressing feature of the factual details surrounding the stories of British POWs at Auschwitz is the apparent total disinterest shown to survivors by the British government. This ambivalent attitude to the Tommy Atkins of World War Two was nothing new and indeed, no doubt existed prior to 1815 when this nickname for the British soldier first originated.

In July 1944 more than one hundred and fifty MPs of all political persuasions in the House of Commons laid down a motion that a minister be responsible for the well being of the POWs returning from Germany. It was put upon the order paper reading as follows: 'That this House, being conscious of the disquiet felt by relatives of prisoners of war and believing that the present system of divided responsibility is unsatisfactory, urges that a senior minister should be designated to co-ordinate and be responsible for all action in connection with prisoners of war and to answer questions.' Colonel Gluckstein (MP for Nottingham East) went on to say that with the scores or even hundreds of thousands of prisoners of war and, if one included in the total their relatives and families, it was a very much larger concern and one that could cause considerable problems. Coupled with the number of government departments concerned in the care and welfare of prisoners of war, there was plenty of room for over-lapping, confusion and even conflict. It was vitally necessary to achieve a closer co-ordination without delay.

Major Sir Jocelyn Lucas (Portsmouth South), as one who was in German prisons and hospitals for four years during World War One and was connected with societies for the rehabilitation of returning prisoners, supported Gluckstein strongly. More support came from Lieut.-Colonel Sir Thomas Moore (Ayr Burghs) who congratulated Lucas on the restraint that he showed with a subject which had aroused if not passion then certainly a great deal of emotion. He added that the question of returning POWs and their problems of resettling into civilian life, not to mention the effects on their families, made this issue truly a national one and therefore one that should be given special treatment. That, of course, reinforced the suggestion that these cases should be in the hands of one responsible Minister. Sir Thomas went on to say that he did not like committees very much because they were apt to be a method of evading direct personal responsibility. Considering the fact that many thousands of our young men would be returned to us probably mental and physical wrecks, the existence of this special Minister would be vital.

Mr Tinker (Leigh) was also supportive of Gluckstein and stated that the Labour Party would favour his idea. Several times he had tried to find out about prisoners of war but on each occasion had been unable to get any information, having been directed to the Red Cross. He conjectured that hardly seemed the way to do it, and there ought to be some responsible Minister to whom people could appeal, for the prisoners of war had a special claim on this country.

Mr Geoffrey Hutchinson (Ilford) backed the motion in order to improve matters in general, with the existing arrangements having produced overlapping, confusion and conflict. He went on to say that an uneasiness undoubtedly existed in the mind of the public that in some way the prisoner of war was falling between two stools, and that his needs were being neglected because responsibility for his welfare was divided between a number of different agencies.

Miss Ward (Wallsend) laid great emphasis on the fact that the government were perfectly satisfied with the present position but, there again, had been satisfied ever since the beginning of the war. The fact that a very large number of names appeared as backing this Motion on the Order Paper is an indication that the House felt the government's attitude was not in fact representative of the views of the people and that the anxiety in the country had grown. She added that when she was on journeys abroad she received from senior officers in the Forces great criticism of the War Office's handling of prisoner of war matters.

The Rt. Hon. Clement Attlee, Lord President of the Council, answered that 'the wrongs it is sought to right are largely illusory'. The families of some of those British POWs returning from German camps in 1945 merely received a letter from the War Office warning them that their returning family member might be slightly odd for a while. Returning

POWs like Arthur Dodd were even deducted wages for allowing the Germans to take and keep their webbing and rifle whilst in captivity and afterwards. To further rub salt in the wound, some years later the German government handed over one million pounds to Britain as compensation for British POWs – not one penny of which ever reached a deserving recipient. It is a shameful but nevertheless true statement to make that Britain treated its servicemen, who sacrificed so much, so shabbily. Any German POW camp represented an exceedingly grim prospect to any inmate, but for the British Government to classify all enemy camps merely as 'German camps' showed a total ignorance of the fact that Brits were also incarcerated in Auschwitz. With inhumane atrocities meted out to the Jews on a daily basis, the British internees were eyewitnesses to these darkest scenes, the most horrific crime of all time. When compared to the average German detention camp anywhere on mainland Europe, Auschwitz was in a league on its own, unparalleled in the depths of depravity to which it descended.

It might be assumed that the British government knew nothing of their countrymen being detained at this epitome of evil in Polish Silesia, and that Clement Attlee was equally ignorant of the fact as late as November 1944. Otherwise one would think they would be more considerate to men exposed at first hand to inhumanities which would traumatise and mentally destroy them either there and then or, more commonly, in later life.

However, the National Archives have yielded document HW 1/761, a copy of an intercept of Nazi communications passed to Churchill in July 1942, a full eight months before Arthur Dodd was to tread those bloodstained acres. The intercepted German Police communiqué 34/42 read as follows: 'Eighty British prisoners (Haeftlinge) suitable for employment as 'Capos' are required for the concentration camp at Auschwitz (Schlesien). ('Capos' appear to be overseers or foremen selected from among the prisoners themselves.) Message dated 23/6/42.' This proves conclusively that the British government was aware that British POWs were imprisoned at Auschwitz during the war. Without doubt, all the more shame should be heaped on the government of that day and all the subsequent governments who collectively did nothing to help young men come to terms with their visions of obscenities. Many died horrible deaths from being traumatised by the pictures that just would not leave their minds, especially in later life.

In marked contrast to the indifferent attitude exhibited by his country of birth, the State of Israel duly acknowledged Arthur risking his own life in assisting Polish Partisans to attempt to cut the wire at Birkenau and promote a Jewish breakout. The Holy Land Foundation presented a Tree Certificate to the Cheshire man with the following citation:

> Trees have been planted in the British Park at
> Hevel Adulam on the Judean Plain, Israel in
> the name of ARTHUR DODD.

Two accompanying statements were also on the certificate:

> One that saves one human life
> is as though they have saved the human race.
> But one that destroys one human life has
> destroyed the world
>
> (Talmud)

> And when you come into the Land you shall plant
> all manner of trees...   Leviticus xix 23

EPILOGUE

On 31 December 1999, the dawn of a new millennium, *Fantasy Feast 2000* was published with all author royalties going towards the Save the Children fund. Those involved were from the ranks of the rich and famous; hundreds of leading personalities from the worlds of music, art, literature, politics, fashion, sport, design, science, film, TV and radio. Also included was Arthur Dodd. The premise of the book was that each person could invite whomever they liked to a special fantasy millennium party at a venue of their choosing.

Predictably, Arthur chose the gas chamber at Auschwitz as his location. His guests were divided into two categories, hearts of stone and hearts of gold. The former group consisted of Adolf Hitler, Heinrich Himmler, Dr Josef Mengele, Gertrude Klink and Rudolf Hess. Their menu offered Buna potato soup and water. The hearts of gold included Primo Levi, Maria Kostka, Anne Frank, Leon Greenman, medical officer Captain Spencer and finally Corporal Purdy. They enjoyed caviar and champagne.

The special Cheshire man listed his greatest achievements as being his unshakeable faith, his family and his forgiveness.

LEST WE FORGET

From Auschwitz archives together with some names kindly provided by surviving POWs, below is a list of the British and Commonwealth soldiers forced to witness the unspeakable horrors of the Final Solution.

Though the list is far from complete, their names form part of our country's history and may enable a grieving relative to draw strength and pride from a loved one's contribution to the attempt to sabotage the efficiency of the Nazi regime. The general resilience of the British lads, their will to keep fighting the war behind enemy lines, together with their downright cussedness, were a constant hassle to the Third Reich. Sitting out the war was never on their agenda, yet their bravery has received little post-war press. This book seeks to fill some of that void.

(D) signifies those killed during the first American air raid on the factory on 20 August 1944, when 38 POWs were killed in total.

Adams, Bill
Adkin, John Henry
Allan, Robert H.
Allingham, Harry

Andrews, Bill
Aplin, Wilhe
Ault, B. T.
Avey, Denis
Bagshaw, Harold
Bamford, William
Bartell, Ernest
Battams, Alfred
Baxter, R.
Beattie, Scottie
Berry, David
Best, John
Birch, C.
Bishop, Brian
Black, Michael (D)
Blades, Alan
Bond, Douglas
Bosworth, Thomas Richard
Boulton, Ken
Bowden, Dick
Boxall, Ron
Bragg, Dave
Brew, Allen
Brown, Charles
Brown, Frank (D)
Buckley, Basil
Burn, Norman
Burns, Harry
Campbell Private
Cane, William

Carr, Reginald David (D)
Cawdeary, Bill
Chalkley, Fred
Chapman, Robert
Charters, Horace
Christian, Reg
Clarke, William (D)
Clatterbridge, ?
Clegg, A.
Cockerell, Ted (Australia)
Colville, Dan
Cook, Bent (South Africa)
Cooper, H. (Titch)
Corbett, Albert
Corrin, George
Cossar, Robert
Costen, Jim
Coward, Charlie (Second Camp Leader, Camp VI)
Cummings, Corporal
Curry, Tommy
Curtis, Reginald
Cuthbert, Harold
Dales, Leonard
Dando, Archie
Daniels, J. W.
Davidson, James
Davis, W. N. (New Zealand)
Davison, Fred
Deakin, W. K. (New Zealand)
Denton, Alf

Deponio, Joe
Dingham, Tommy
Dinnie, J.
Dodd, Arthur
Dodds, Sid
Doyle, Eric
Driscol, William
Duffree, George
Ellison, Ron
Farrar, Tommy
Fawcett, Stan
Ferencz, Ben
Ferris, Robert
Firth, Ray
Fleet, Jimmy
Fowler, G.
Frost, Douglas Tilbrook
Gaines, Ronald Albert
Galley, Raymond
Gardiner, James William (D)
Gifford, A.
Gifford-England, Arthur H.
Ginn, Frank
Gordon-Brown, L.
Gorman, Terry
Gotch, Walter

nis Arthur

LEST WE FORGET

Harris, Frank
Harrison, Capt. (South Africa)
Hartland, Reginald
Hartree, Ernest Arthur (D)
Harvey, Don
Hatch, W. J.
Hawker, Bishop
Haywood, William Charles (Charlie)
Hedges, Bill
Herring, Frederick (D)
Hicks, Allan L.
Hill, Charles
Hinds, Frank
Hornfield, Stanley
Horton, Jack
Howard, Major (Camp Leader, Camp IV or VIII)
Howe, Eric
Howells, W.E.
Howse, Bob
Hughes, Frederick (D)
Hunt, Steve
Hutch, W. J.
Ingman, J.
Innes, Sergeant Major (First Camp Leader, Camp VI)
Jobling, R.
Jones, Bob
Jones, L.
Jones, Ron
Jordan, William (South Africa)
Keegan, Andy

Keenan, Titch
Knight, John
Lambkin, Jack
Lark, W.
Lea, William
Ledger, Steward
Lee, 'Taxi'
Lemin, Bill
Lepinnet, A.
Lewis, Albert
Lindsay, Eric
Livingstone, Ernest
Longden, George Harry
Longold, L.
Lougher, Albert (Australia)
Lovell, Kenneth Clifford
Lowe, Regimental Sergeant Major
Lucy, Lyle
McElwee, William
McPherson, James
Magee, John
Maltby, J. E.
Marshall, Jack
Martin, Walter
Mathews, Sidney Edward (D)
Meredith, Bill

hilip (D)

Milton, John
Monaghan, Patrick
Mulligan, John T.
Murphy, Charlie
Murphy, Terry
Murray, John
Murray, Fred
Norman, Frank
Ogden, Harry
Oldham, George
O'Mara, George
Osborne, Dr Spencer Ian
Ovenstone, Jock
Owen, Reg
Panayoton, George
Parr, W. E.
Parry, 'Ginger'
Parry, Thomas
Pascoe, John
Percy, Gilbert (D)
Piddock, Charlie
Pike, Johnnie
Pitt, Archie
Powell, Sandy
Presson, Samuel (D)
Price-Williams, William
Purdy, Jim
Quartermaine, Cyril
Randall, George (South Africa)
Redding, William Jesse (D)

Redman, Ronald
Reeves, Eric
Regan, John (D)
Renshaw, Bill
Reynolds, Leslie
Ridd, Albert
Ridgers, Richard
Roberts, Sidney
Robertson, Robert, RAMC
Rolls, Ivor Herbert
Rush, Harold (D)
Sanders, Samuel (D)
Satterthwaite, John
Saunders, George Alexander
Scott, W.
Seal, Albert Victor
Sevenoaks, George
Shaw, Edward
Shaw, 'Liverpool'
Shepherd, Clifford
Simpson, Jimmy
Simpson, 'Yorkshire'
Smith, A. H.
Smith, Jim
Smith, Peter (D)
Snape, Albert

Stevens, John (Jack)
Stirling, James
Stow, Alfred C.
Sykes, Albert
Szweda, Stan
Taylor, Tommy
Trusty, Jack
Walker, Jack
Walton, Henry
Waring, Pongo
Ward, Bill
Ward, Thomas
Watts, Robert Alfred (D)
Wellard, R. J. F.
Whiffin, Richard
White, Blanco
White, Frederick George (D)
Wilkins, A.
Williams, Tom
Wiper, William Rye (D)
Wise, A. E.
Wooley, Frederick
Woolley, Vic
Wright, Syd
Young, Raymond (D)

Arthur Dodd wishes to acknowledge the following people who helped him to make it against all odds.

Medical Officer Captain Spencer
No Doctor was filled with more caring.

Corporal Purdy
A Saint among men in everything he did.

Corporal Cummings
Always there for others.

Sergeant Andy
He'd walk a million miles to motivate others to do seven hundred.

Taffy the Choir
This perfectionist helped sanity in making others reach for his goals.

Sergeant Major Charlie Coward
Wheeler dealer working against the Nazis.

God Bless them all!

Foreword by Major General Patrick Cordingley, DSO, FRGS

EYEWITNESS TO WAR

THE FINEST WRITING ABOUT WAR BY THOSE WHO WERE THERE

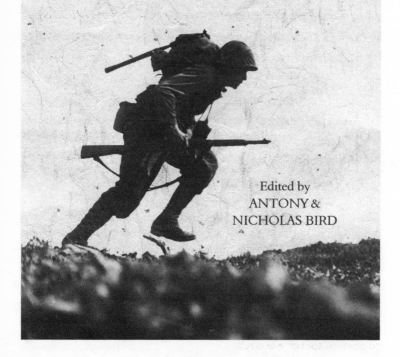

Edited by
ANTONY &
NICHOLAS BIRD

EYEWITNESS TO WAR
The Finest Writing About War by Those Who Were There

Antony & Nicholas Bird

£9.99

ISBN: 1 84024 543 3
ISBN 13: 978 1 84024 543 1

Hardback

'In the finest tradition of Palgrave's Golden treasury, this historic collection of war inspired prose and verse may be seen as an extremely worthy attempt to bring together the "best of the best"'   History.uk.com

The inescapable irony of war is its ability to inspire the finest and most poignant literature. In the tension and drama of battle, in the terror and pathos, all man's senses are engaged and heightened. Few settings kindle the poetic spirit more fiercely than the battlefield, while facing both the enemy and one's own mortality.

Gathered within this book is an extensive collection of some of the most vivid and eloquent prose and verse from those who, throughout history, have witnessed the intensity of war at first hand. Beginning with Elizabeth I's stirring speech to her soldiers at Tilbury as the Spanish advanced across the Channel, and ending with the devastation surrounding the overthrow of Saddam Hussain's Iraqi dictatorship, each piece is introduced by a penetrating and original analysis of the story behind the words, offering a stirring and moving glimpse of the consuming soul of war itself.

The AGE of SCURVY

How a Surgeon, a Mariner and a
Gentleman helped Britain win the
Battle of Trafalgar

STEPHEN R. BOWN

THE AGE OF SCURVY

How a Surgeon, a Mariner and a Gentleman Solved the
Greatest Medical Mystery of the Age of Sail

Stephen R. Bown

£7.99

ISBN: 1 84024 402 X
ISBN 13: 978 1 84024 402 1

Paperback

'The Age of Scurvy *is a gripping book and a bargain, full of adventure, big
events and human nature at its best and worst*'
New Scientist

'*A startling look at ignorance, courage and determination*'
The Good Book Guide

From the sixteenth to the eighteenth century, one dreaded foe was
responsible for more deaths at sea than piracy, shipwreck and all other
illnesses combined. This scourge of the seas was Scurvy. Countless
mariners perished from an agonising death which began with bleeding
gums, wobbly teeth and the opening of old wounds.

Surgeon James Lind, sea captain James Cook, and physician Sir Gilbert
Blane determined to crack the riddle of Scurvy. Their achievements
heralded a new era and solved the greatest medical mystery of the
Age of Sail.

Stephen R. Bown is an award winning historical writer whose articles
have appeared in Canada's national history magazines. His first book
was *Sightseers and Scholars: Scientific Travellers in the Golden Age of
Natural History*.

www.summersdale.com